D1193027

CALIFORNIA DREAMIN'
ALONG ROUTE 66

On the Cover: The Will Rogers Highway Association never missed a chance to promote Route 66 as the route to the sunshine, glamour, and pretty girls in California. Press releases and promotional photographs of models posed on the beach or along the road, many in high heels, were issued constantly. These models, whose names were not recorded, were posed ever so naturally along Santa Monica Boulevard prior to one of the annual Will Rogers Highway Association conventions. Will Rogers helped promote Route 66 throughout his career and planned to retire to his ranch near Santa Monica before his life was cut short in a plane crash.

CALIFORNIA DREAMIN'
ALONG ROUTE 66

Joe Sonderman

ARCADIA
PUBLISHING

Copyright © 2019 by Joe Sonderman
ISBN 978-1-4671-0316-9

Published by Arcadia Publishing
Charleston, South Carolina

Printed in the United States of America

Library of Congress Control Number: 2018964819

For all general information, please contact Arcadia Publishing:
Telephone 843-853-2070
Fax 843-853-0044
E-mail sales@arcadiapublishing.com
For customer service and orders:
Toll-Free 1-888-313-2665

Visit us on the Internet at www.arcadiapublishing.com

*In memory of Lillian Redman, Bob Waldmire,
Gary Turner, Bill Shea, and Laurel Kane.*

CONTENTS

ACKNOWLEDGMENTS

I could never do a single book without the help of Cheryl Eichar Jett, Mike Ward, and Steve Rider. Special thanks go to Jim and Judy Hinckley. I had extra help this time from the following California experts: Scott Piotrowski, Dan Rice, and Michael Boultinghouse, who knows all about the National Old Trails Road. Thanks are also owed to Blue Miller, Caltrans, Anthony Reichardt, and the National Park Service's Route 66 Corridor Preservation Program. Authors Jerry McClanahan, Jim Ross, Shellee Graham, Russell Olsen, Quinta Scott, David Wickline, and of course, the great Michael Wallis blazed the trail, and their works are always valued references. See you on the road!

Unless otherwise noted, all images are from the author's collection.

INTRODUCTION

The California dream made Route 66 the most famous road in the world. Route 66 brought several distinct waves of migrants that transformed the state. They fled from the ravaged Dust Bowl in the 1930s, and another wave came seeking defense plant jobs during World War II. Prosperity and new attractions brought both permanent residents and vacationers after the war.

Native Americans had been using this pathway for thousands of years when the first extensive American travel and trade to Southern California came over the Mojave Indian Trail, the Old Spanish Trail, and the Mormon Road.

In 1857, Lt. Edward Fitzgerald Beale led an expedition to establish a wagon road along the 35th parallel between Fort Smith, Arkansas, and the Colorado River and then through the old trails across the Mojave. Beale and his men used camels as pack animals. The Santa Fe Railroad, Route 66, and Interstate 40 generally followed this corridor.

When the Santa Fe arrived, the railroad established water stops across the desert roughly every eight miles and named them in alphabetical order starting with Amboy and continuing with Bolo, Cadiz, Danby, Essex, Fenner, Goffs, and so on east to Needles. Primitive desert roads stuck close to the rails.

In 1895, the state legislature created the Bureau of Highways, and two years later, California became the second state to form a highway department. In 1910, the first state route ran between Placerville and Lake Tahoe, later US 50. California voters approved the first highway bond issue to establish 3,000 miles of state roads, which included sections that became US 66.

The first section paved, located between Los Angeles and San Bernardino, was done under a state contract from 1913 to 1915. The road between San Bernardino and Cajon Summit received a macadam surface in 1916. Another 26 miles of pavement between the summit and Victorville were completed in 1920, leaving 26 miles of dusty trail to Needles.

During the 1910s and 1920s, private promoters were busy mapping out a confusing array of routes bearing fancy names across the country. But many promoters spent little on maintenance and routed hapless motorists many miles out of their way to a town or business that paid to be on the route.

The National Old Trails Road was more legitimate. It ran across the Mojave and through the Cajon Pass to Los Angeles. Sen. Harry Truman of Missouri was the head of the National Old Trails Association, the only such group authorized by an act of Congress. The Automobile Club of Southern California led the way as well by signing the great transcontinental routes.

In 1925, the US government formed a committee under the Department of Agriculture to create a numbering system for federal routes. The committee assigned even numbers to the east-west highways, with the important transcontinental routes ending in "0." Cyrus Avery of Tulsa, Oklahoma, used his influence to route the Chicago–Los Angeles highway through his hometown. It was not a true transcontinental route, but Avery's road was assigned the number 60. Some states even printed maps showing US 60.

But Kentucky governor William J. Fields protested, demanding that Route 60 pass through his state. The committee relented and assigned the number 62 to the Chicago–Los Angeles route; however, Missouri and Oklahoma officials balked at that. A standoff ensued until Oklahoma's chief engineer John M. Page noticed that the catchy-sounding "66" was unassigned. Meeting in Springfield, Missouri, on April 30, 1926, Avery and Missouri officials agreed to accept 66. The new federal system went into effect on November 11, 1926.

However, the National Old Trails Road name just would not go away. It was still signed and shown on maps, and much of the public continued to use the term for years to come. The Route 66 shields would not appear in some areas until 1929. The last portion of Highway 66 to be paved in California ran for 30 miles between Essex and Klinefelter and was completed in 1931. This new section provided a shorter route and made Goffs one of the first Route 66 towns to be bypassed.

The road through the Cajon Pass was widened and realigned between 1932 and 1934, and a section was relocated after a flood in 1938. Widening of Foothill Boulevard between San Bernardino and Pasadena began in 1930. Two sections were realigned in 1932, and it was four lanes wide by 1938.

Route 66 became ingrained in pop culture because it had its own publicity machine. The US 66 Highway Association put out a steady flow of press releases, and the nation followed an epic transcontinental footrace, nicknamed the "Bunion Derby," along the entire length of 66 in 1928. More publicity came when Los Angeles hosted the Olympics in 1932. The US 66 Association advertised that 66 had more paved miles than the other route.

Images of overloaded jalopies will always be associated with Route 66 in the 1930s. In *The Grapes of Wrath*, author John Steinbeck called Route 66 "the Mother Road . . . the road of flight." As the migrations reached about 100,000 per year, the refugees were derided as "Okies" and faced open discrimination. In 1936, the Los Angeles Police Department went so far as to establish a "bum blockade" at the state lines.

The original route from Colorado Boulevard in Pasadena headed south on Fair Oaks Avenue to Huntington Drive and then turned onto Broadway. A 1931–1934 alignment used Fair Oaks, Mission Street, Arroyo Drive, Pasadena Avenue, and York Drive through Highland Park, turning south to follow the west bank of the Arroyo Seco along Figueroa Street. A temporary route in 1935 passed through Eagle Rock. Beginning in 1936, the alignment shifted to drop down from Colorado Boulevard to North Figueroa Street. Also in 1936, the route was extended west along Sunset Boulevard and Santa Monica Boulevard, but it never officially reached the ocean.

The first portion of the Arroyo Seco Parkway opened in 1940. The first limited-access freeway in Los Angeles, it carried Route 66 until 1964, when the route over Figueroa was designated as US 66 Alternate.

The years after World War II were the glory days of Route 66. Nat King Cole recorded "(Get Your Kicks on) Route 66," and the middle class hit the road in record numbers. Many headed for Disneyland, which opened in 1955. But Route 66 was becoming a victim of its own success—it was clogged with traffic and dangerous. Limited-access freeways made it obsolete.

In 1953, the Hollywood Parkway, as it was first known, connected to the Arroyo Seco Parkway in Los Angeles at a four-level interchange. The freeway replaced the portions of US 101 and US 66 along Sunset Boulevard. The route through Cajon Pass was widened and improved between 1952 and 1955.

In 1956, Pres. Dwight Eisenhower signed the Interstate Highway Act, authorizing $26 billion to construct 41,000 miles of limited-access highways across the nation. By this time, Route 66 had been transformed from a mere highway to a symbol of freedom and adventure, tinted by nostalgia. From 1960 to 1964, that image was bolstered by the CBS television series *Route 66*.

Route 66 was eventually replaced by Interstates 40, 15, 210, and 10 across California. The route was officially decertified in 1985, but it would not die.

Today, there are countless books, guides, and websites devoted to Route 66. The old road is more than just cracked pavement and nostalgia. While travelers on the freeway blast through unaware of their surroundings, the Route 66 adventurer reconnects with the communities. They meet people with diverse viewpoints and lifestyles. Adventure is waiting at the next freeway off-ramp.

One

ACROSS THE MOJAVE

The Atlantic & Pacific Railroad, later the Santa Fe, constructed the Red Rock Bridge over the Colorado River in 1890. From the time a flood wiped out the ferry in 1914 until the Old Trails Bridge opened in 1916, vehicles crossed on planks laid over the rails during the times between trains. Highway 66 moved from the Old Trails Bridge to this structure as of May 21, 1947. Abandoned after Interstate 40 opened in 1966, the Red Rock Bridge was demolished in 1978.

The Old Trails Bridge opened on February 20, 1916, and was featured in the film *The Grapes of Wrath*. At 800 feet, it was the longest arch bridge in America, but it could carry only one lane at a time. After the Santa Fe opened a new double-tracked railroad structure in 1945, work began to convert the Red Rocks Bridge to carry Route 66. The deck was removed from the Old Trails Bridge, and it carries a natural gas pipeline today.

Travelers stop for a photograph on the California side of the National Old Trails Bridge. Dust Bowl refugees might have been disheartened by their first view of the promised land, as another mountain range and the Mojave Desert were still ahead. In *The Grapes of Wrath*, Tom Joad says "This here's a murder country. This here's the bones of a country." The original Route 66 wound up the hill but was chopped up by Interstate 40.

Needles, California

Originally a mining and railroad town, Needles was established in 1883 and named after the jagged peaks of the Black Mountains. This old borax wagon was used in the 1940 film *20 Mule Team* and then served as the sign for the El Rancho Needles Motel. It was donated to the city in 1962 and restored in 1986. Route 66 originally followed Front Street, K Street, and Spruce Street to the Needles Highway. The later route followed Broadway.

Carty's Camp was first encountered by westbound travelers arriving in Needles and was also briefly visible in *The Grapes of Wrath*. Bill Carty and Dick Mansker opened the camp in 1923, and it grew to include 12 cabins and a motel, called the Havasu Court. Carty retired in 1948. He sold to Charles Canterbury and Loren Ames, who operated the station as the C and A Chevron. The station is boarded up, but some of the abandoned cabins remain.

Adjacent to Carty's Camp, the Route 66 Motel in Needles was constructed in 1946–1947. The six-room motel faded after Interstate 40 opened about a mile away in 1973. Marjud Paakanaan from Finland managed to keep it open and in good shape through the late 1990s, but it has been operating as apartments for years. The sign was relit on June 23, 2012, after Ed Klein of Route 66 World raised funds and worked on its restoration.

Orsavella and Charles Fahey's Needles Campground was located at a sharp turn on the west side of town. The gas pumps were repeatedly demolished by errant drivers. The couple were divorced in 1933 and Orsavella married Guy Austin in 1936. The cabins were moved to a former railroad tent camp at Broadway and Front Street that they renamed the Palms Motel. It was the Old Trails Inn from 1991 to 1997, when the cabins were renovated for monthly rentals.

H-2233 EL GARCES, FRED HARVEY HOTEL, NEEDLES, CALIFORNIA

Fred Harvey hotels and restaurants brought civilization to the dusty towns along the Santa Fe Railroad. The El Garces location at Needles opened on April 3, 1908. It was named for Fr. Francisco Garces, a missionary, and designed by Francis W. Wilson. The Harvey House closed in 1949 and was used as offices for the Santa Fe Railroad until 1988. Vandals and weather took their toll, but the extensively renovated El Garces reopened as an intermodal transportation facility in 2014.

The Needles Theater was constructed in 1929 to house a Masonic temple on the top floor. It was designed by local architect DeWitt Mitcham. The first level housed a sweet shop, a real estate business, and the theater. The theater opened on March 1, 1930. It could seat 700 people and had a water-based heating and cooling system. The building was closed following a fire in 1992 and sat vacant for years. Part of the roof was blown off in 2012, but restoration efforts continue.

Needles became a major stop for travelers on Route 66 before the trek across the Mojave Desert. The Art Deco facade of the Claypool department store building is visible on the left in this view of Broadway and D Street. It opened in 1930, and the facade was covered up with a modern design in the 1950s. The original front has been restored and the building is used by Palo Verde College. The Imperial 400 Motel stands on the site of the Texaco station today.

Alexander and Grace Swain's motel had 32 units located at Broadway and B Street, one-half block off Route 66. Swains Motel was operated by Peg, Mike, and Perry Phillips at the time of this postcard. It became the El Vee Motel in the 1960s. In the late 1990s, the fire department used it for training. Colorado River Plumbing stands here today. Other motels in Needles included the Del Rhea, the Sage, Overland, River Valley Motor Lodge, Kiva Motel, and the Desert Inn.

Sarah and Robert Robertson came from Scotland and in 1928 opened the Robinson Motor Inn on F Street in Needles. They located their two-story home in the middle and surrounded it with eight tidy Bungalow-style cabins with private garages. Shown here in 1941, it later became known as Robinson's Motel. By the 1950s, the sign out front advertised "Air Conditioned for Your Comfort by York." It still stands as the Robinson Apartments. Note the post office across the street.

Imperial 400 Motels were known for their wing-shaped roofs, designed by the architectural firm of Palmer and Krisel. The chain was founded in Los Angeles in 1959 and started out opening a new location every 10 days. By the time the chain went bankrupt in 1965, there were 85 of them, including Route 66 locations at Needles, Barstow, and Pasadena, California; Albuquerque, New Mexico; and Flagstaff and Kingman, Arizona. The Needles location is still there.

Early travelers on Route 66 dreaded the Mojave Desert and often stayed in Needles or camped beside the Colorado River during the day to attempt the desert crossing at night. In his 1946 *A Guide Book to Highway 66*, Jack Rittenhouse warned motorists to carry extra water for the car and noted that "skeletons of abandoned cars are frequent by the roadside." This 1957 photograph was taken when the Chevrolet station wagon shown was two years old.

During World War II, over a million soldiers trained in an 18,000-square-mile area of the Mojave Desert in California and Arizona in preparation for desert warfare in North Africa. Camp Essex, Camp Clipper, and Camp Ibis were in the Needles area. In *Guide Book to Highway 66*, Rittenhouse wrote that signs warning of mines and unexploded ammunition were common. These troops were reviewing the results of maneuvers near Needles in 1942. (US Army.)

Highway 66 climbs over 2,200 feet over a 27-mile stretch of searing desert from Needles to Mountain Springs Pass, once the location of the Mountain Springs Auto Camp. Once motorists reached this point, it was another 135 miles across the desert to Barstow. Water was sold by the gallon here unless gasoline was purchased. The remnants of the Mountain Springs Auto Camp were demolished for the construction of Interstate 40.

In December 1931, Route 66 was relocated away from the railroad onto a more direct route between Needles and Essex. Goffs thus became one of the first Route 66 communities to be bypassed. This Mission-style schoolhouse, built in 1914, closed in 1937. Restored by the Mojave Desert Heritage and Cultural Association, it now houses a museum. Between US 95 and the Mountain Springs Road Exit, Interstate 40 follows the post-1931 route. (Mike May.)

Essex had the most services for motorists between Amboy and Needles, including a free drinking fountain erected by the Automobile Club of Southern California. The Wayside Camp, shown here in 1932, was purchased by O.B. Chambers after World War II. There was no television in Essex until 1977, when a few residents went on *The Tonight Show Starring Johnny Carson* and a company offered a signal translator at no cost.

Essex marks the turnoff to Mitchell's Caverns in the remote Providence Mountains State Recreation Area. They were opened to tourists in 1933 by Jesse Estes "Jack" Mitchell. He and his wife, Ida, lived in the home shown and survived hard times during World War II when the Army closed off access. Jack died in October 1954 when a vehicle he was repairing for an unsavory character mysteriously fell off the jack. The caverns were sold to the state. (Steve Rider.)

Between Essex and Ludlow, a levee running along Route 66 was designed to divert water away from the roadway and into the dry washes during desert downpours. For many years, the earthen berm has also provided a canvas for roadside artwork as travelers leave their names spelled out in rocks, cans, bottles, and other roadside debris. Bob and Bud left their mark and photographed their handiwork here in 1956.

After nursing their overheated vehicles to the pass through the Marble Mountains, motorists were glad to see the café, service station, and garage at Cadiz Summit. Thomas R. Morgan ran a store in Amboy before establishing Cadiz Summit in 1928. George Tinken was the owner from 1936 until 1942. Dick and Nadine Cruse were the last in a series of other owners. Cadiz Summit closed soon after Interstate 40 opened, and only a few graffiti-covered ruins remain.

James Albert Chambless and his wife, Fannie, ran a station and store on the unpaved National Old Trails Road that became US 66. The windmill on the right pumped water at this remote location, and the sign at center advertised free maps of "the Main Street of America." Route 66 was realigned just to the south in 1932, so James and Fannie opened the Chambless Camp at the junction of the new paved highway and the road south to Cadiz. (Steve Rider.)

The Chambless Camp was a rare shady spot in the Mojave Desert because the main building had a huge canopy over the pumps. James died in 1940, and Fannie Chambless sold to William and Wilma Riddle in 1944. Their son Jack sold it to Steve and Lorraine Stephens in 1965. The area is known as Chambless but the Cadiz Post Office was located here for a time, causing some confusion. The canopy is gone, but the main building and the cabins still stand.

Road Runner's Retreat at East Amboy is a picturesque ruin from late in the Route 66 era. Retired driver Roy Tull and his wife, Helen, opened the truck stop in 1962. The restaurant was leased for a time by Duke Dotson. It is another example of a business that closed after Interstate 40 opened, although Road Runner's Retreat briefly came back to life for the filming of a Dodge commercial in 1988. The sign and ruins are fading in the brutal desert sun.

In 1883, Lewis Kingman of the Atlantic & Pacific Railroad, later the Santa Fe, mapped out the water stops across the Mojave Desert in nearly alphabetical order from Amboy to Needles. That gave us Bolo, Cadiz, Danby, Essex, Fenner, Goffs, Homer, Ibis, Java, Klinefelter, and so on. Amboy was established in 1858 as headquarters for salt-mining operations. Development of the National Old Trails Road and Route 66 made it an important stop for travelers.

In 1938, Roy Crowl opened his service station and café at Amboy, where water had to be brought in by train. Herman Bazel "Buster" Burris became a partner when he married Crowl's daughter Betty. Burris bought the complex from his father in law and constructed or owned much of the town. Roy's was busy around the clock and had 70 employees in a town of 700 people. But it all faded rapidly after Interstate 40 opened in 1973.

The iconic sign at Roy's was added in 1959. The complex also became a popular filming site for car commercials and music videos. Buster Burris charged exorbitant prices and was known to chase away rowdy bikers or visitors he deemed undesirable at the point of a gun. Roy Crowl died in 1977 and Burris bulldozed much of the town to avoid paying taxes. He leased out what was left and retired in 1995, then sold it all just before he died in 2000.

The second wife of Buster Burris, Bessie, regained ownership of Amboy in 2003 and offered the entire town for sale on eBay with an asking price of $1.9 million. There were no takers. In February 2005, Albert Okura, owner of the Juan Pollo restaurant chain, offered $425,000 in cash to the Burris family and promised to preserve the town and Roy's. On April 28, 2008, Roy's reopened offering a few basic items after $100,000 in renovations and repairs.

Roy's was not the only stop in Amboy. Ben Benjamin's station, café, and cabins became Bender's One Stop, operated by brothers Martin and Joe Bender. The Amboy Post Office was located at the complex. The Benders sold to Constantinos "Conn" and Lillian Pulos in 1948, and the business was renamed Conn's. Luther Friend rebuilt after the main building burned down in the 1960s. Fire destroyed the shuttered business after Interstate 40 was completed.

An extinct volcano can be seen from Route 66 a short drive west of Amboy. The volcano that formed Amboy Crater was last active about 10,000 years ago. It left behind a 43-square-mile lava field that was used to test one of the Mars rovers, and the cone was featured in the 1959 film *Journey to the Center of the Earth*. In the 1940s, pranksters set debris on fire in the crater, making it appear as if an eruption was imminent. A trail leads 3.5 miles to the rim, but the summer heat is deadly.

Bagdad began as an important railroad stop and is known for the longest drought in US history, 767 straight days from 1912 to 1914. Alice Lawrence ran the Bagdad Café from the late 1940s through the 1950s and inspired the movie *Bagdad Café* and the short-lived CBS show. The café closed in 1968, and in 1991, a natural gas company used the site to store pipes and destroyed all traces of the café. The movie was filmed in Newberry Springs. (See page 28.)

Siberia was little more than a Santa Fe Railroad watering siding with an exotic name. Like the other stops strung out across the Mojave Desert, it faded quickly after the switch from steam to diesel engines. The Siberia Texaco station and its tiny garage served motorists along Route 66. The foundation ruins remain, along with some of the white-painted stones that were used to line the driveway.

Ludlow, named for a railroad car repairman, boomed when gold was discovered nearby in 1900. The town was the terminus for the Tonopah & Tidewater Railroad, serving the borax mines and the Ludlow & Southern that ran to the gold mine. Brothers Tom and Mike Murphy owned a good portion of the town. As mining declined, the Murphys and others opened new businesses just north of the old town to serve National Old Trails Road and then Route 66 travelers.

Mathilde "Ma" Preston, the imposing owner of the Ludlow Mercantile, feuded with Tom and Mike Murphy. She accused them of overturning a barrel while she was bathing in it! She sued but settled out of court after Mike Murphy reacted to a string of her invective by hitting her with a hose coupler. In 1920, Ma Preston sold to her bitter rivals and retired to France. The store ruins partly collapsed during an earthquake in 2008. (Steve Rider.)

Built partly of lumber salvaged from the Tonapah & Tidewater Railroad, the streamlined Ludlow Café was operated by Rex and Lilian Warnix for 20 years. Laurel and Cameron Friend then operated it until 1975, three years after Interstate 40 opened. The abandoned building remained standing but was gutted by fire and demolished in 2015. A café with the same name remains in business in an A-frame building off Interstate 40.

A National Old Trails Road guide described the landscape between Ludlow and Barstow as "practically level, broken occasionally by dry lakes, extinct volcanic craters and mountain ranges in the distance." These August 1927 photographs show that improvements to the roadway east of Newberry were already underway. In 1930, Route 66 was moved to the north. The rugged old segment shown here looking east still exists, but it was never paved. (Both, Caltrans.)

Newberry Springs was simply called Water by the Santa Fe Railroad because there is plenty of water underground. The precious fluid was shipped to remote eastern Mojave stops by rail. It became Newberry in 1911 and changed to Newberry Springs in 1967. There were once plenty of services for travelers here, but the Cliff House had a public swimming pool and the only phone in the area until the mid-1950s. The main building still stands. (Steve Rider.)

It was set in Bagdad, but director Percy Adlon filmed *Bagdad Café* in Newberry Springs at the Sidewinder Café. The 1987 film became a cult favorite in Europe, but the owner made the movie company restore the nondescript Sidewinder after filming. The Pruett family brought back the film version and changed the name to Bagdad Café after they became the owners in 1995. Andree Pruett now greets visitors from around the world. (Jim and Judy Hinckley.)

The National Old Trails Road and the original US 66 turned sharply to cross the Santa Fe tracks at Minneola, midway between Newberry Springs and Daggett. This August 1927 photograph shows the dirt roadway improved with a "super elevated curve" at the crossing. In 1930, Route 66 was realigned to stay south of the tracks. On the north side of the tracks, the original route follows Santa Fe Street between the Barstow-Daggett Airport and the town of Daggett. (Caltrans.)

Dust Bowl refugees faced the fear of being turned back at the agricultural inspection sites in California. The stations were set up to keep out harmful pests from fruits and plants, but were often used to keep out people deemed undesirable. The Daggett station is shown here in 1930. It was relocated east of town and expanded before being shown in *The Grapes of Wrath*. The facility that still stands near the Barstow-Daggett Airport opened in 1953 and closed in 1967.

Daggett was once a rough town where the 20-mule teams unloaded borax and loaded supplies for Death Valley. Originally known as Calico Junction, it was renamed for John Daggett, the lieutenant governor of California who platted the town. Homer Cameron Ryerson's General Store was rebuilt with concrete after a fire in 1908. Now the Desert Market, it is the only store for miles around. The old pool hall and Stone Hotel (1883) are next door. (Jim Hinckley.)

Located 22 miles west of Ludlow, the original Mojave Water Camp dated to the days of the National Old Trails Road. Ed Poe bought it around 1940. He removed the awning, changed the brand to Shell, and added Poe's Café next door. A new station was later constructed and Gen. George Patton is said to have visited the café when his troops were training nearby. Poe's evolved into the Desert Oasis, a name that lives on at the nearby Interstate 40 rest area. (Edgar Poe Jr.)

Two

THE HIGH DESERT AND CAJON PASS

BARSTOW, CALIF. 6067

Barstow was first known as Waterman Junction, and the name was changed in honor of Santa Fe Railroad president William Barstow Strong in 1886. His middle name was used because there was already a Strong Station in Kansas. Originally, the business district was in front of the Harvey House on the other side of the tracks. The Santa Fe expanded its yards in 1925, and the businesses were rebuilt two blocks to the south along Main Street.

Casa del Desierto in Barstow was the pride of the Fred Harvey system when it opened on February 22, 1911. It replaced the original structure that burned in 1908. Casa del Desierto closed in 1971, was abandoned, and then severely damaged in a 1992 earthquake before the City of Barstow began restoration. It now houses the Amtrak stop and the Western America Railroad Museum. The Mother Road Route 66 Museum is also located there.

The Fred Harvey company recruited white women "between the ages of 18 and 30, attractive, intelligent and of spotless character" to serve guests. The famous Harvey Girls, shown here at Casa del Desierto, worked long hours in starched black and white uniforms and were paid $18.50 per month plus room, board, and tips. The girls had to adhere to a strict code of conduct and a curfew. They were pioneers in a time when few women worked outside the home.

Smoke rises from trains in the Santa Fe yards in this view of El Rancho in Barstow. Ed Chase built the motel in 1947 using railroad ties salvaged from the Tonopah & Tidewater Railroad. The 100-foot-tall neon sign drew travelers from miles away, and El Rancho was a popular stop for Hollywood stars. It closed in 1979, housed railroad employees for a time, and then fell into disrepair. Rick Byers restored it twice, but part of the complex was damaged by fire, and it has faded again.

The Cactus Motel, located at 916 East Main Street in Barstow, was built in 1949 and still stands with its vintage sign intact. There were plenty of motels in Barstow, where US 66 and 91 met at an intersection with five service stations. The city is still a major transportation hub as Interstates 40 and 15 meet at the east end of town. Two major transcontinental railroads move freight through Barstow, the Union Pacific and the Burlington Northern & Santa Fe.

Sands Motel
924 E. Main Street (U. S. 66), Barstow, Calif.

The couple who mailed this postcard from the Sands Motel in Barstow to back home in Ohio on July 6, 1957, reported that it was 126 degrees in Needles the previous day and was still over 100 degrees when they came through at midnight. They arrived in Barstow at 4:00 a.m. and said it was so hot they could hardly stand it, adding "Ohio is a nice place to live." The Sands at 924 East Main Street is still there, and the vintage sign is mostly intact.

West Barstow was growing rapidly in the 1940s and developed its own business district, shown here looking west. At left are Jim Kail's Auto Court and the Retzlaff Pontiac dealership. The Oasis Café is visible on the right and the tiny Desert Trading Post was next door. The café site later became Carlos and Toto's and the Costa Azul Restaurants, but a new complex housing Desert Ambulance Services is located here today.

In 1929, the Richfield Oil Company built a chain of 125-foot-tall aviation beacons spaced about 50 miles apart from Mexico to Canada. Huge neon letters on each tower spelled out "Richfield." The company planned to build hotels under some of the beacons. The Beacon Tavern at Barstow opened on June 27, 1930. Due to the Depression, it was the only hotel Richfield constructed. It was a busy stop until Interstate 15 opened in 1958 and was demolished in 1970.

Frank Woods subdivided a large plot of land in 1924 and named it Lenwood Estates after his wife, Ellen. They partnered with a shady character who sold the lots while promising improvements that were never made. But Lenwood prospered anyway, appealing to those seeking "suburban desert living." The Radio Auto Camp billed itself as the "coolest spot on the desert" and even had a beer garden. A single building remains today. (Steve Rider.)

In 1941, Spanish-American War veteran Guy Wadsworth constructed William "Bill" and Alice Potapov's station east of Oro Grande. Bill and his family took over in 1943, and Alice ran a lemonade stand out front. When motorists could not pay for repairs, Bill took non-vital parts off their cars as collateral. The station had been abandoned for many years when a new owner bulldozed the ruins in September 2007. (Anthony Reichardt.)

MOTOR INN AUTO COURT AND TRAILER PARK
HIGHWAYS 66-91, ORO GRANDE, CALIF.

Oro Grande was another mining town with a name that literally means "great gold." In the 1950s, Truman "Warren" Finney's Motor Inn Auto Court and Trailer Park was the only motel in town. Most of it still stands, tucked away amid a scraggly group of trees. Out on the road, a figure of a multicolored cow atop Cross Eyed Cow Pizza overlooks the railroad, and the antique shops seem to run the entire length of town.

As a child, Elmer Long and his father collected bottles and other items from old mining town dumps. Elmer turned their lifelong interest in relics into a folk art display west of Helendale; he created a forest of metal and glass known as the Bottle Tree Ranch. Amid the 200 colorful bottle trees that Elmer welded together are all manner of repurposed desert castoffs, including road signs, guns, insulators, and even a traffic light. Elmer often greets travelers marveling at his work.

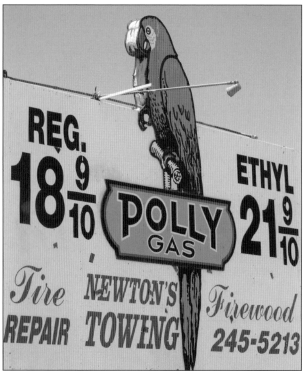

Prices on the sign at the site of the Polly Gas station remain frozen in time. Annette and Bill Watson made bricks by hand to build their garage on the east side of Route 66. Polly Gas was their second business, located about a mile to the north on the west side. Annette somehow kept an eye on four kids while selling gas at the station, and Bill worked at the garage. Both businesses closed after Interstate 15 opened. (Jim Hinckley.)

Officially named the Rockfield Bridge, the span carrying Route 66 between Oro Grande and Victorville opened in February 1931 and is one of the most unique on the route. It crosses the Mojave River at one of the only places the elusive stream flows above ground year-round. The steel Baltimore truss structure is skewed to cross the river at an angle, and is also notable for its ornate railings. It was bypassed in 1972 but still carries traffic today.

Roy Rogers, the "King of the Cowboys," and his wife, Dale Evans, appeared in dozens of films and owned the Double R Bar Ranch off Route 66 in Oro Grande. Their museum on Route 66 in Victorville is a lost roadside attraction. The collection was moved to Branson, Missouri, in 2003 and that museum closed in 2010. But a likeness of Roy's famous horse, Trigger, still rears up on the neon sign for the New Corral Motel in Victorville.

Victorville was originally known as Mormon Crossing and then became Huntington Station, a railroad stop. It was changed to Victor in honor of California Southern (Santa Fe) Railroad's construction superintendent Jacob Nash Victor. However, there was already a Victor in Colorado, so it became Victorville in 1901. While the Stewart Hotel is gone, the California Route 66 Museum is located a block away in the town's first bank building, built in 1918.

GREEN SPOT MOTEL Victorville, Calif. 44108 Houck-Corona

John Roy built the Green Spot Motel at Victorville in 1937. Kay Aldridge, an actress known for the 1942 serial *Perils of Nyoka*, bought the complex in 1982. She sold to Benjamin Wu and Nancy Wei just a few weeks before Wei was convicted of killing her husband. The motel fell on hard times, but by 2018, it had undergone some repairs and sported a new paint job. A broken sign out front still reads "Nyoka's Hideaway."

"THE GREEN SPOT CAFE" TOURIST HEADQUARTERS - VICTORVILLE, CALIF.

The Green Spot Café played a major role in motion picture history. In 1940, Orson Welles banished alcoholic writer Herman Mankiewicz to Victorville to work on the screenplay for *Citizen Kane*—free from the distractions of Hollywood. Under the supervision of Welles's collaborator John Houseman, Mankiewicz was allowed one drink each night at the Green Spot bar while writing the first two drafts. The café burned in 1953.

KLEEN SPOT
AUTO COURTS

ON HIWY. 66 WESTSIDE
VICTORVILLE, CALIF.

There were just 10 units at the Kleen Spot Motel in Victorville. A café was also part of the complex at 15370 Seventh Street. When a truck slammed into the café in 1962, the cook prepared the driver a sandwich and then shut the place down for repairs. The old motel and the café building are still recognizable today. The café is now listed as Papi's Auto Detailing, and the motel has been converted to apartments and no longer looks very "Kleen."

In 1947, Bob and Kate Holland opened the Holland Café in Victorville. During his 30-year career driving a cement truck, Richard Gentry ate at the café often and bought it in 1979. He named the café for his wife, Emma Jean, who had worked as a waitress there. Emma Jean died in 1996, and Richard died in 2008. His son Brian Gentry and Brian's wife, Shawna, run the business today. The Holland Burger Café was featured in the movie *Kill Bill: Volume 2*. (Blue Miller.)

The Outpost Café at the junction of Highways 66 and 395 opened in 1928. George Newton and his family bought it in 1961. When the state condemned the property for highway expansion in 1964, the family was offered just $600 in compensation. The Newtons won a larger settlement in court and then opened a big café and truck stop nearby. The former café became the Outpost Wedding Chapel and stood for many more years on a dead-end section of old pavement.

The original Summit Inn was located at the junction of the 1916 and 1923 alignments of the National Old Trails Road in Cajon Pass and opened in 1928. When Route 66 was realigned in 1930, the inn was relocated a short distance away and was known as Harrison's Summit Inn Café, as shown here. When the highway was realigned in 1952, Burton and Dorothy Riley opened the third incarnation of the Summit on the east side of Route 66.

When the divided roadway opened, the third Summit Inn ended up on the west side of the highway. Elvis Presley stopped here and was irked that none of his records were on the jukebox. His waitress said he tipped well. Cecil Stephens ran the Summit Inn from 1966 until 2016, when Katherine Juarez and her brother Rocino took over. The Blue Cut fire wiped out the Summit Inn on August 16, 2016, but reconstruction was underway in 2019.

Native American trails in the Cajon Pass between the San Bernardino and San Gabriel Mountains were followed by the Old Spanish Trail, the Salt Lake (Mormon) Trail, and a toll road opened in 1861. A narrow gorge created here by Cajon Creek is called the Blue Cut for the color of the rocks. The new 3.8-mile section of Route 66 shown here looking south from the summit opened in May 1931 and had to settle before paving. The cut has been widened substantially.

The roadway in the Blue Cut, present-day Cajon Boulevard, crosses the San Andreas Fault and was very prone to landslides. A section originally part of the National Old Trails Road was realigned in 1932. By the time this photograph was taken in June 1938, the state was finishing up work on a retaining wall to protect the roadway. Two new lanes were built to carry northbound traffic in the 1950s, and Interstate 15 came through in 1969.

Christianson's Cajon Mountain Camp was located at the "Y" intersection of Route 66 and CA 59, today's interchange of Interstate 15 and CA 138. It was owned by Carl and Cleo Christianson. In 1943, they sold to William and Aleta McSwain. Edna and Jim Dyer leased it from 1948 to 1950, when it was torn down for construction of the rerouted Highway 66. The site is now the northwest part of the interchange. (Steve Rider.)

Constructed by William Marion Bristol, Camp Cajon was an early welcome station on the National Old Trails Road in Cajon Pass, dedicated on July 4, 1919. Camp Cajon was destroyed by a flood on March 2, 1938, but some of the big stone picnic tables were brought to San Bernardino at Perrish Hill and Lytle Creek Parks. Bristol was a firm believer in euthanasia. When he became ill in 1941, he built his own coffin, climbed in, and shot himself.

Ezra Meeker came west over the Oregon Trail as a youth and retraced the journey several times in his late 70s to make sure the trail was not forgotten. His son Marion established a store, garage, and camp in 1919 and also became the caretaker of Camp Cajon. Louis Palmer owned the station at far left and then bought out the Meekers in 1929. Marion and his brother Ezra then opened a new complex and the Sunrise Cabins to the north. Palmer's was wiped out in the 1938 flood. (Steve Rider.)

Located where Route 66 met the Wrightwood Road, the second incarnation of Meeker's opened in 1929. On April 11, 1945, a runaway truck, hauling 21,000 pounds of meat and 8,100 pounds of butter, slammed into Meeker's at 100 miles per hour. The driver died when he jumped out after failing to bring the vehicle under control. These buildings were leveled, but Ezra Meeker and his first wife, Frances, somehow escaped injury. The truck just missed their bed. (Steve Rider.)

After the runaway truck disaster, the Meekers built a modern café, shown here, but this incarnation had to be demolished for construction of the four-lane Highway 66 in 1954. Ezra combined two surviving cabins into a home and then opened the Double D Ranch Café and a small station on a new site just to the south. It was in business until Ezra died in 1966. His second wife, Mabel, lived in the home until 2002. (Steve Rider.)

Three

THE INLAND EMPIRE

Route 66 follows Cajon Boulevard through Devore and enters San Bernardino on North Mount Vernon Avenue. John Russo built the Mount Vernon Motel at the intersection of Cajon Boulevard and Mount Vernon Avenue. The building permit issued in 1940 called for 19 rooms, but by the summer of 1941, there were 60 units with garages adjoining the stucco cottages. The motel still stands and has been converted to apartments.

Brothers Richard and Maurice McDonald converted their barbecue restaurant at Fourteenth and E Streets (City 66) into a hamburger stand in 1948. Milk shake–mixer salesman Roy Kroc was impressed by the efficient assembly line technique and began franchising McDonald's in 1955. Kroc bought out the brothers for $2.7 million in 1961 and eventually ran them out of business. Their restaurant was razed in 1972, but the site is now a museum celebrating the fast-food giant.

San Bernardino is the last city listed in "(Get Your Kicks on) Route 66." Composer Bobby Troup once said, "I could have put in those other cities, but it would have made the song too long." (Los Angeles is mentioned in the line "It winds from Chicago to LA.") San Bernardino had a motel named after the Mother Road. Opened in 1946, the Motel 66 at Mount Vernon Avenue and West Fourteenth Street no longer stands.

In the 1960s, Virginia Arness, former wife of *Gunsmoke* actor James Arness, operated the Oasis Motel in San Bernardino. In October 1967, she was profiled in *Ebony* magazine for running one of the first integrated motels in that area. She called it a "citadel of love," and according to the magazine, it was popular with artisans. The Oasis is still in business. The sign originally had a figure in a turban on top, but it was removed years ago.

The Mission Auto Court was one of the first elaborate motels in California. Clarence E. Howard envisioned a chain of similar courts when he opened the original 22 stucco units in 1929. It was constructed on the former estate of Aaron Cox, owner of vast citrus groves. W.D. Fisk began expanding in 1935, and it eventually grew to 70 units. The fire department burned the condemned motel down for practice in August 1984.

Mission Auto Court — "One of the Best in the West"; 1150 Mt. Vernon Avenue, San Bernardino, Calif.

The Gateway City   'Phone 33208 — Thos. I. Proctor, Prop.   65039

Franciscan missionary Francisco Dumetz of the San Gabriel Mission arrived in present-day San Bernardino County on May 20, 1810, the feast day of St. Bernardine of Siena. A Mormon colony purchased the Rancho San Bernardino in 1851. They laid out the town based on Salt Lake City, and Pioneer Park marks the original town square. San Bernardino grew in importance when the Santa Fe Railroad arrived in 1886. This view looks north on E Street downtown.

San Bernardino's Santa Fe station was once the largest railroad depot west of St. Louis. The Mission Revival–style depot opened on July 18, 1918, and replaced the original that burned down in November 1916. The San Bernardino Associated Governments took over the station in 1992, and restoration began in 2002. The station now serves an Amtrak Line and two Metrolink commuter lines. It also houses the San Bernardino History and Railroad Museum.

From 1934 to 1964, City Route 66 used Kendall Drive to E Street. These specially built General Motors Futurliners are passing Pioneer Park on E Street on February 8, 1956. They were part of the GM Parade of Progress, a traveling road show that was making a stop at the Orange Show Grounds. The 12 Futurliners were built in 1940. Nine of them survive, but only three have been restored, with one selling at auction for $4.1 million in 2006. (General Motors.)

GATE CITY AUTO COURT, opposite National Orange Show, SAN BERNARDINO, CALIFORNIA

The Gate City Auto Court stood at the busiest intersection in San Bernardino, where Mill Street, E Street, and Colton Avenue (now Inland Center Drive) met at the entrance to the National Orange Show. Al and Opal Heckman bought the court just six weeks before it was devastated by the deadly flood of March 2, 1938. It reopened in mid-May 1938, and Sally Douglas sold it to Virgil Whitman in 1944. The structures were demolished in 1964. (Mike Ward.)

EIGHTEENTH NATIONAL ORANGE SHOW, SAN BERNARDINO, CALIF.   FEB. 16-26, 1928.

San Bernardino businessmen created the National Orange Show to boost the citrus industry, and the first one was held in two tents on a vacant lot in 1911. A huge exposition building at Mill and E Streets opened in 1925. The shows once drew 300,000 people during the annual two-week run. The hall burned down in 1949, and the show became more of a traditional fair with less emphasis on citrus. The 100-acre National Orange Show Events Center is now a year-round venue.

Comic and philosopher Will Rogers made his last public appearance at the California Theater in San Bernardino on June 28, 1935. On August 15, he died in a plane crash with famous aviator Wiley Post in Alaska. The Art Deco theater on Fourth Street opened on August 15, 1928, with a sold-out showing of *Street Angel*, starring Janet Gaynor. It is now the California Theatre of the Performing Arts.

In 1937, Lucia Montano opened the Mitla Café in a former drugstore on North Mount Vernon Avenue. Glenn Bell owned a burger and hot dog stand across the street and learned how to make hard-shell tacos at the Mitla. Bell opened the first Taco Bell at Downey, California, in 1962. The Mitla is still an important part of the Mexican American community in San Bernardino. From left to right are Vera Montano Lopez, Maria Olave, and unidentified. (Mitla Café.)

From Mount Vernon Avenue, Route 66 originally turned west on Fourth Street and curved onto Foothill Boulevard headed toward Los Angeles. That was before a bridge was constructed on Fifth Street over Lytle Creek in 1931. This view is looking east on Foothill Boulevard at the Fifth Street Split in 1938. The sign at the Richfield Stations is a smaller replica of the big beacons the firm erected at locations such as the Beacon Hotel in Barstow.

Motorists through San Bernardino often found their way blocked by trains until the I Street Overhead opened on September 10, 1951. Looking east from J Street, the driveway at right led to the Santa Fe Railroad emergency hospital. The current bridge over the tracks, and Interstate 215, was dedicated in 2009 in honor of John Knabenbauer. The Caltrans worker was struck and killed while removing an obstruction on Interstate 215 in November 2007. (Caltrans.)

A model poses poolside at the Motel San Bernardino, which is still in business today at 2528 East Foothill Boulevard. At the west entrance to town, it retains its attractive vintage sign. The motel was operated by Lloyd Kernkamp when this photograph was taken. As of 2018, some Route 66–era motels that remain in San Bernardino include Andy's Motel (now the Lido Motel), the Valley Motel, the Motel Holiday Inn, and the Motel Dream Inn with its pretty orange-and-blue sign.

Frank Redford said that, as a boy, he lived on a Sioux reservation, which provided some of the inspiration for his patented chain of motels resembling wigwams. The Wigwam Motel at the San Bernardino–Rialto line was the last of the seven he constructed. San Bernardino city planners rebuffed Redford when he first proposed construction in 1946. Work started in September 1949, and the 11 original stucco-clad wigwams opened in April 1950. Eight more were added in 1953.

The Wigwam Motel began to fade after the Foothill Freeway was constructed in 1958. By the 1970s, the rooms were rented by the hour, and the sign out front read, "Do It in a Tee Pee." In 1989, the owner even sought a permit to tear it down. The Patel family bought the rundown landmark in 2002 and began a long and expensive effort to save it. The Wigwam remains a Mother Road treasure.

Rialto was one of a string of 25 stations established when the railroad was constructed between San Bernardino and Pasadena in 1887. In *Guide Book to Highway 66*, Rittenhouse wrote of this area, "You will pass through 12 small communities before reaching Pasadena. Many of these are so close together as to be practically indistinguishable from each other." Explosive growth transformed Rialto in the 1950s. (Steve Rider.)

Four

ACROSS THE FOOTHILLS

Fontana was born on June 7, 1913, when about 4,000 people came out to see one of the largest private land developments in the history of the West. Azariel Blanchard Miller planned the community to include the world's largest citrus grove and 75 miles of streets. It remained mostly rural until World War II, when Henry J. Kaiser decided to locate a massive steel plant on the site of a hog farm, spurring migration to the area. (Steve Rider.)

The Kaiser Plant made steel plates for the West Coast shipping industry during World War II and the Korean War. Employment at the plant peaked at 13,000 in the early 1970s. After Kaiser went bankrupt in 1983, much of the plant was dismantled and reerected in China. Another large portion was demolished for the California Speedway. Other parts of the complex can be seen in films such as *Terminator 2* and *Independence Day*. (Fontana Historical Society.)

Vineyard owners Jim and Frances Bono opened a produce and orange juice stand on Foothill Boulevard in Fontana on July 17, 1936. They constructed a restaurant building in 1943, and Bono's became one of the best-known Italian restaurants on Route 66. The original orange-shaped stand is long gone, but owner Joe Bono saved one from demolition and brought it to the site in the 1990s. The orange is still there.

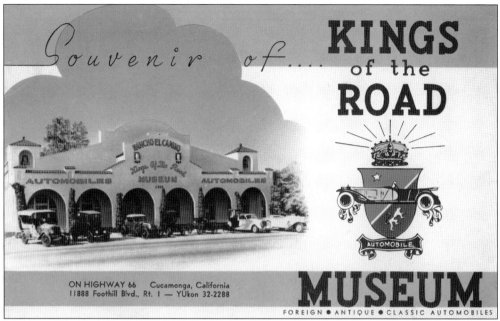

Collectors Dr. Orris R. Myers, Purcell Ingram, and Orville Race established the Kings of the Road Museum in 1954. It was located in a former winery packinghouse at Foothill Boulevard and Rochester Avenue. Eva Braun's 1938 Horch, Clara Bow's Rolls Royce Phaeton, and Jack Benny's Maxwell were also displayed. The collection was later sold to casino magnate William Harrah. The site is now the Old Spaghetti Factory and the Home Depot parking lot.

In its heyday, the Virginia Dare Winery was one of the largest in America. It was originally the Mission Winery, built in 1910 and patterned after the Mission Inn in Riverside. The Garrett Company took over in 1918 and changed the name. The winery was abandoned in 1961, and the ruins served as a set for television shows such as *Combat* and *Rat Patrol*. The original main tower and grape-crushing building were incorporated into an office and retail complex in the 1980s.

Looking east on Foothill Boulevard before Archibald Avenue in Cucamonga, Lucy and John Nonsenzo's Café and the Public Market at right became Carl's Liquor and The Deli. The Union service station is a parking lot, and Bob Ford's Texaco is now Bank of America. At left are the Ancil Morris Richfield Station, Bank of America, and Cucamonga Drug. In 1977, the towns of Cucamonga, Etiwanda, and Alta Loma became the City of Rancho Cucamonga.

Harry Klusman built the Spanish Colonial–style Cucamonga Station on the Old Trails Route for William Harvey in 1915. Harvey sold in 1925 to Richfield distributor Ancil Morris. Arvid Lewis, the first Cucamonga fire chief, owned the station from 1945 until 1971, when it closed. The Route 66 Inland Empire California Association began restoration in 2013, and the station was dedicated as a museum on December 12, 2015. (Route 66 Inland Empire California Association.)

Before the Cucamonga Station was constructed, Hugh Lawson's Ford Repairing occupied a large wood-framed building on the site. That structure was moved to the back of the lot and remodeled when the station was constructed, becoming the garage and service bays as shown here. This structure collapsed during a storm in 2010 and was removed. The Route 66 Inland Empire California Association hopes to someday replicate the garage on the site.

The Cucamonga Rancho Winery is the oldest in California. Its roots go back to 1839, when the governor of Alta California granted 13,000 acres to soldier, politician, and smuggler Tiburcio Tapia. It was purchased by Hugh and Ida Thomas in 1918, and Joseph Filippi and family took over in 1967. Very little of the original adobe and brick remained after a 1969 flood, but it was rebuilt. The main building became a restaurant and independent winery.

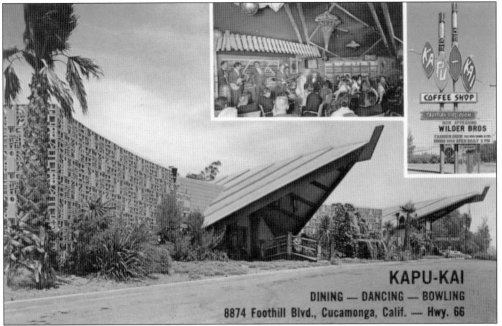

KAPU-KAI
DINING — DANCING — BOWLING
8874 Foothill Blvd., Cucamonga, Calif. — Hwy. 66

A Polynesian paradise once stood next to the oldest winery in California. The tiki-themed coffee shop and bowling alley Kapu-Kai (the name supposedly means "Forbidden Sea") opened in 1962. On January 25, 1969, floodwaters raged through the Kapu-Kai and the Thomas Winery. The Kapu-Kai was abandoned, became the Roller City skating rink, and then was abandoned again. A supermarket stands here today.

Nicknamed "Red Cars," the Pacific Electric Railway interurban system spurred development of communities between Los Angeles and San Bernardino. The last Red Cars line shut down in 1961. The Pacific Electric crossing over Foothill Boulevard east of Upland was built in 1914. It was replaced in 2010 by a new span with a Main Street of America theme. This portion of the old line is now part of the 21-mile-long recreational Pacific Electric Trail. The top photograph was taken in 1914. (Route 66 Inland Empire California Association.)

The oldest restaurant on Route 66 was originally the Mountain View Inn, a stage stop in a sycamore grove established by William "Billy" Rubottom in 1849. Billy Rubottom brought opossum to Southern California and served them up at the inn. Citrus grower and vintner John Klusman built the current structure in 1920. In 1936, Irl Hinrichson named it the Sycamore Inn. Chuck and Linda Keagle took over in 2002 and carry on the tradition of hospitality today.

Next to the Sycamore Inn, the Red Chief Motel opened in June 1936. The 16-unit motel, restaurant, and cocktail lounge at 8270 Foothill Boulevard was operated by Hoyt E. Milton. Milton also owned the Ontario Hotel. It became the Sycamore Motel in 1962 and closed in 1977. The motel units in a semicircle out back were demolished around 1998. The café building last housed a sushi restaurant and was demolished in 2018. (Steve Rider.)

Lucy and John Nonsenzo moved from their café at Foothill Boulevard and Archibald Avenue to run Lucy and John's Italian Dinners across from the Sycamore Inn. John Clearman rebuilt after this building burned in 1955. He drew the name Magic Lamp from a container filled with suggestions by employees. Clearman sold to Frank and Edith Penn, and the Magic Lamp was later operated by Anthony Vernola, who retired in 2012. The sign is notable for its open flame.

The historic Anza Trail, Mojave Trail, Emigrant Trail, and Colorado Road all met at present-day Euclid Avenue and Foothill Boulevard in Upland. There, a *Madonna of the Trail* statue was dedicated on February 1, 1929. It is one of 12 monuments placed in each of the states along the National Old Trails Road to honor pioneer women. The Madonnas were commissioned by the Daughters of the American Revolution and created by sculptor August Leimbach.

On June 3, 1938, Gov. Frank F. Merriam dedicated the final link of the four-lane Foothill Boulevard. The dedication took place at the *Madonna of the Trail* statue. Foothill Boulevard became the longest four-lane highway in California at the time, stretching 28 miles between San Bernardino and the Los Angeles County line. Hundreds of palm and eucalyptus trees lining the route were replanted. (Caltrans.)

Retired college professor George Carter Griswold started selling preserves in 1909 and built a factory and stand at Claremont in 1915. Alton and Betty Sanford bought it in 1950 and added a bakery and smorgasbord, moving across the road in 1960. A motor hotel was added in 1968. They turned the former Claremont High School into a shopping plaza and opened a dinner theater in the old gym. Griswold's closed in 1993, and the motel became a Doubletree.

Isaac Lord of Los Angeles convinced the Santa Fe Railroad to extend its line through his large land holdings and laid out a town he modestly named Lordsburg. Voters changed it to La Verne after he died in 1917. Harry and Cora Belle Wilson converted a big fruit stand just inside the city limits into a sandwich shop in 1930. It became Wilson's Dinner House in the 1950s and closed in 1962. Joe Parker established the landmark La Paloma Restaurant here in 1966. (City of La Verne.)

The original Route 66 went through downtown Glendora, via Amelia Avenue and Foothill Boulevard, jogging south on Citrus Avenue to meet Foothill Boulevard again. In 1933, the route shifted to the new Alosta Avenue, which was rededicated as Route 66 in Glendora on July 14, 2001. The Golden Spur Restaurant at Highway 66 and Hunter's Trail started out in 1918 as a ride-up hamburger stand for customers on horseback. The steak house opened in 1954. It closed in October 2018.

ALBOURNE RANCHO CITRUS STAND
1114 Highway #66 East of Glendora, Calif.

Enormous citrus groves once spread out along Route 66 between San Bernardino and Pasadena. There were dozens of roadside stands, such as this one at the Albourne Rancho. Arthur Bourne, heir to the Singer Sewing Company, owned the citrus ranch and packing plant. The land was subdivided in 1949. In 1968, Michael Rubel began building a folk art castle on part of the old citrus ranch property. It is made out of bottles, rocks, and other salvaged items.

Frank Chance from Glendora became famous as part of the "Tinker to Evans to Chance" double-play combination when he played for the Chicago Cubs. As manager, he led the team to world championships in 1907 and 1908. In 1912, he constructed this building at Foothill Boulevard and Michigan (now Glendora) Avenue in his hometown. The businesses were the Cub Pharmacy, the Cub Grocery, and the Cub Delicatessen. The building was restored after a fire in 1990. (Glendora Historical Society.)

After World War II, Americans took to the road en masse, and many had a trailer hooked up to the family car. In 1948, Henry M. Hanson began making Love Bug trailers in Glendora. Love Bugs were 10 to 22 feet long and included an icebox, stove, sink, and a dinette that converted into a bed for as low as $635. It could sleep four, but there was no bathroom. Wally Byam, who created the famous Airstream trailers, once worked for Henry Hanson. (Steve Rider.)

After leaving Glendora, both Route 66 alignments merge at Foothill Boulevard and Alosta Avenue, where the double marquee of the old Azusa Foothill Drive-In is a landmark. The drive-in opened on December 18, 1961, with showings of *Babes in Toyland* and *Misty*. It closed on December 28, 2001, after the land was purchased by Azusa Pacific University for a parking lot. The university agreed to refurbish and maintain the marquee.

Azusa is named after the Native American village Asuksa-nga, and the local chamber of commerce promoted it as having "Everything from A to Z in the USA." Englishman Henry Dalton acquired the land in 1844 but lost most of it to banker John Slauson, who laid out the town in 1887. The city hall and civic center complex has changed little from the days when "Anaheim, Azusa and Cuc-a-monga" was a punchline on *The Jack Benny Program*, a radio show. (Mike Ward.)

M-5   FOOTHILL BOULEVARD, AZUSA, CALIF.

The plaque on this monument at the intersection at Foothill Boulevard and Azusa Avenue was dedicated to the World War I veterans from "the Canyon City" in September 1923. The monument was demolished after the road was widened in July 1946. Since August 1947, a replica of the plaque has stood on the lawn at the Azusa Civic Center. The city has erected modern gateway monuments, based on the original design, along three major travel corridors.

This McDonald's at 568 East Foothill Boulevard in Azusa, the eighth in the nation, opened in September 1954. Architect Stanley Clark Meston was hired after others rejected Richard and Maurice McDonald's ideas. Meston was offered a one-time payment or a commission for each new McDonald's. He chose the single payment. This location closed in 1984 and was demolished in 1989.

Foothill Boulevard becomes Huntington Drive at the San Gabriel River Bridge. Albert C. Mayer of Los Angeles and his wife decided to start a business in the country in 1920, which was about the time a beekeeper relative died. Suddenly, they were in the honey business. The Mayers spent six weeks sorting through boulders on the property to construct Honeyville, and 600 colonies of bees kept the honey flowing. The business moved to Durango, Colorado, in 1954.

The Hi-Way 66 Foothill Motel at 2435 East Foothill Boulevard (now Huntington Drive) opened about 1947. It had 25 concrete cottages with individual garages and was owned by Mr. and Mrs. F.R. Braune. By 1958, it had become the Capri Motel, which was demolished for a housing complex in 2013. The couple who sent this postcard wrote that their green 1946 convertible with a black top, shown here, was sold to Honest John's Used Car Lot in Las Vegas.

In 1841, the governor of Alta California granted former Mexican army corporal Andres Duarte 7,000 acres, which he named Rancho Azusa de Duarte. Other towns created from the grant include Bradbury, Monrovia, Azusa, Irwindale, Baldwin Park, and Arcadia. "Sweetest on 66" was the motto at the Casa Bonita Motel on Huntington Drive in present-day Duarte. This postcard puts the Casa Bonita in Monrovia because it was printed before Duarte was incorporated.

The Motel Yearling at 151 East Huntington Drive in Duarte was owned by Abe and Mary Doornbos. It was originally the Motel Porter. Yearling refers to a young horse, as the motel was a 10-minute drive from the Santa Anita Racetrack. The Yearling is now the Rancho Inn, which is the only surviving classic Route 66 motel in Duarte. The sign with the horse head has been replaced with a modern sign and the new name.

The Trails Restaurant became a landmark before Duarte even officially existed. Bill and Edith Brothers opened it on August 31, 1952. Edith and her co-owner Robert Basha closed it down in 2001. Despite pleas by preservationists and Route 66 enthusiasts, the Trails was demolished for a condominium development. The streets are named for some of the rooms at the Trails, such as Waterfall, Hideaway, and Crossroads. (Route 66 Corridor Preservation Program.)

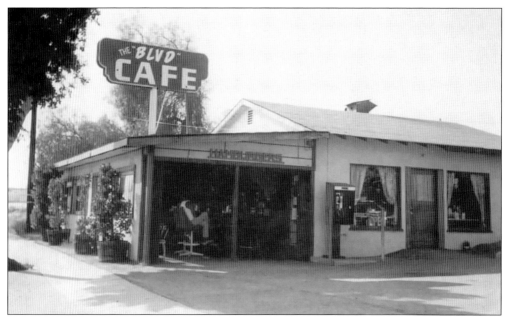

When Suzy and Tommy Tomasian took over a small wooden orange juice and hamburger stand in 1946, they had to decide on a new name that would fit on the sign. So, it became the Blvd. Café. It was still in the family in 1989, when the Duarte City Redevelopment Agency used eminent domain to acquire the property. The family received $1.1 million for a lifetime of memories, and the building was torn down for a shopping center.

CHAPEL INN
DUARTE, CALIFORNIA

The Chapel Inn was originally All Saints Episcopal Church, built in 1896. Clarence and Delia Gordon bought the building for their restaurant in 1926. As a show of respect to the history of the building, they would not sell alcohol. Patrons included Clark Gable, Claudette Colbert, Jean Harlow, and Bette Davis. The American Legion bought the former church in the 1960s. An effort to raise funds to preserve the former chapel failed. (Mike Ward.)

Sportsmans Tavern
1452 Huntington Drive
Duarte, California

Guests enjoyed wild game raised on the site at the unique Sportsman's Tavern, at 1452 Huntington Drive in Monrovia. It was established in 1932 by Ethel Maskey, who served in France with the Red Cross during World War I. The property included vast pens for rare birds and ponds and pools for frogs, ducks, turtles, and trout. Even the fruit was grown on site. Celebrities like Clark Gable and Errol Flynn ate there regularly. Sportsman's closed in the 1970s.

Located 902 E. Huntington Dr.
Monrovia, California

Abbott's Café was the original business on the southeast corner of Huntington Drive and Mountain Avenue in Monrovia. Sometime in the 1940s, the K.C. Jones Drive-In was built on the site. The back of the postcard advertises: "Specializing in barbecue spareribs, chicken in the basket and shrimp." The location is listed as Monrovia, but the intersection is now inside the Duarte city limits. A gas station is located on the site today.

Looking East
on
Foothill
Boulevard

Monrovia
California

ELEVATION 450 TO
1100 FEET.
MONROVIA LIES
DEEP IN THE
HEART OF SOUTH-
ERN CALIFORNIA
BETWEEN THE
MOUNTAINS AND
THE SEA.

F 8846

Monrovia was once part of two large ranchos, the Azusa de Duarte and Santa Anita. The town is named for railroad builder William N. Monroe, who established the Monroe Ranch in 1884. The original Route 66 turned from Huntington Drive, north onto Shamrock Avenue, and then west on Foothill Boulevard. It then turned south on Santa Anita Avenue to Colorado Boulevard. The post-1933 route skipped the turn to the north and remained on Huntington Drive.

AZTEC HOTEL, MONROVIA, CALIF.

Monrovia's Aztec Hotel opened on September 6, 1925. Robert Stacy-Judd designed the hotel in Mayan style but insisted it be called the Aztec because the Mayans were not as well known. The Hollywood elite frequented the Aztec in the years after the Santa Anita Racetrack opened, but it later deteriorated into a flophouse. The Aztec was renovated in 2012, and the Brass Elephant Bar inside was featured in the film *Bad Santa*. (Mike Ward.)

The palm-thatched Wigwam stood beside the original Route 66 alignment via Foothill Boulevard at present-day Wigwam Avenue in Monrovia. It opened in 1920. Hal Slemons, his son James, and the entire "Slemons Tribe" ran the operation, which also included the busy Wigwam brand juice factory in back. The Wigwam went up in flames on January 31, 1935. El Ranchito Spanish Restaurant opened here in 1936, and the site is now a McDonald's.

The Derby Restaurant in Arcadia started as the Proctor Tavern, and moved from Foothill Boulevard to Huntington Drive in 1931. Legendary jockey George Woolf, nicknamed "the Iceman," became a partner in the restaurant in 1938 after riding Seabiscuit to victory over Triple Crown winner Royal Admiral. Woolf was killed during a race at Santa Anita in 1946. The restaurant, featured in the movie *Step Brothers*, still has an amazing display of racing memorabilia.

Legends said the stately and ancient oak in front of the Oakleigh Motel was "the hanging tree" during Monrovia's wilder days. When it became the Oak Park Motel, the owners paid tribute with a neon oak tree on the sign. The Oak Park Motel was demolished after a fire in the 1970s, and the 200-year-old landmark tree came crashing to the ground on October 8, 2014. No one was hurt, but a couple of townhomes on the site were damaged. (Steve Rider.)

These used vehicles are waiting for buyers on the Main Street of America at Bob Longpre Pontiac, 335 West Huntington Drive. Longpre began working on the Pontiac assembly line in Michigan when he was 16. His father, Raphael, was the division production manager. After running a dealership in Massachusetts, Bob took over R.R. Moore's Monrovia location in April 1950. Longpre sold this dealership in September 1966, and it no longer stands. (Steve Rider.)

Back when orange groves lined Route 66, pottery stands were also common. The Pottery Ranch at 248 West Huntington Drive was in business for over seven decades. Opened in 1940, it specialized in selling factory seconds but survived by turning to first-class merchandise at deep discounts. Dottie Kahan became the owner in 1952. The Pottery Ranch lost its lease in 2011 and was demolished for a fast-food restaurant.

Van de Kamp's Dutch-themed bakeries and their trademark windmills were once common across the Los Angeles region. In 1967, the company opened its first coffeehouse with an updated design at Huntington Drive and Santa Anita Avenue in Arcadia. The windmill blades halted in 1989 when Denny's moved in, but public outcry kept them intact. The blades began turning again on June 29, 2016, but had to be repaired after they fell off in December 2017.

Mr. and Mrs. Ben Petre lived in a six-room penthouse atop their Moderne–style Santa Anita Motor Inn. The first motel in Arcadia, it opened in September 1938. Designed to resemble a ship, the motor inn on the northwest corner of Huntington Drive and Santa Clara Street consisted of 15 units surrounding a landscaped courtyard with a beautiful fountain. It closed in December 1973, and skateboarders used the old pool to showcase their skills until the vacant complex was torn down in October 1975.

William Parker Lyon, founder of Lyon Van and Storage and the former mayor of Fresno, California, displayed a vast collection of Western relics from stagecoaches to scalps and Ulysses S. Grant's cigar butts at Lyon's Pony Express Museum in Arcadia. The six-acre museum, located across from the Santa Anita Racetrack, opened in 1934. Lyons amassed the largest collection of porcelain chamber pots in the world and called his autobiography *Pot Luck!*

William Parker Lyon died in 1949, and the museum closed in 1955. His treasures were sold to casino magnate William Harrah, who moved it all to Reno. The collection was broken up and auctioned off after Harrah died in 1978. The Flamingo Hotel, which had live flamingos on the grounds, opened on the museum site in 1956. In 1988, it became the Santa Anita Inn, which was demolished in 2018 for a Marriott hotel project.

Charles and Harry B. Carpenter founded a drive-in restaurant chain, and later, Charles split and opened his own, which included Carpenter's Santa Anitan, pictured here. It opened in November 1939. The logo at left identified the Santa Anitan as a Chicken in the Rough franchise, which was one of the first restaurant franchises. Its eaten-by-hand chicken dinner was developed by Beverly Osborne at his restaurant on Route 66 in Oklahoma City. The restaurant became Henry's Drive-In during the 1950s, and an office building stands here today.

The Westerner Hotel

Swimming Pool of Southern California's Finest New Motor Hotel

Located on Highway 66

ARCADIA CALIFORNIA

Across from the Famous Santa Anita Race Track

E-4-134

Huntington Drive connects with Colorado Place at the Santa Anita Racetrack and Route 66, then merges onto Colorado Boulevard. Walter and Kay Muller's Westerner Hotel at 161 Colorado Place opened in 1947. A trade magazine honored Walter for his "foresight and daring" for making the Westerner one of the first motor hotels with televisions, air-conditioned rooms, and a swimming pool. An office building stands on the site today.

SANTA ANITA RACE TRACK ARCADIA, CAL. 841

Will Rogers was among the 30,777 people on hand on December 25, 1934, for the opening of the new Santa Anita horseracing track. The "photo finish" was introduced at Santa Anita during that first season. The flamboyant Elias J. "Lucky" Baldwin built the original Santa Anita in 1904, but California outlawed horse racing in 1909. Baldwin was well known for his shrewd investments and affairs with many women when he subdivided his land to create the city of Arcadia.

A dark chapter in Santa Anita's history began in March 1942, when nearly 20,000 Japanese Americans were forced into an overcrowded assembly camp surrounded by barbed wire. About 8,500 lived in converted horse stalls that smelled of manure. The internees were moved to permanent internment camps by the end of October, and Santa Anita became an Army training facility. German prisoners of war were housed there later in the war. (National Archives.)

Fantasy Island was on Route 66! The Los Angeles County Arboretum and Botanical Garden has 127 acres of exotic plants, located on part of the old Baldwin ranch. The former ranch guesthouse, the Queen Anne Cottage, appeared on the television show. Visitors can also see a reconstruction of an 1840 adobe home and the Santa Anita railway station. The station was moved piece by piece when the freeway was built in 1970.

Betsy Ann Hisle's star shone briefly on the silver screen, and her likeness showed up on the roadside. Betsy was a child star whose big break came in *The Way of All Flesh*, a 1927 silent film nominated for best picture. Family friend Arthur Hartman banked on her stardom when he built his ice cream parlor at Foothill Boulevard and Michillinda Avenue in her likeness. After Betsy's popularity ebbed, it was renamed the Doll House and, later, demolished.

Charlie Eaton opened his Santa Anita Restaurant in December 1939 on the southeast corner of Colorado Boulevard and Michillinda Avenue, a site once part of the Lucky Baldwin Ranch. A $100,000 motel complex with 60 bungalows on 8.5 acres of landscaped grounds opened in 1941. In 1969, the Internal Revenue Service seized the property for unpaid taxes, and the complex was demolished in 1975. The site became a Coco's Restaurant. This image is from a vintage menu.

Five

PASADENA AND THE EARLY ALIGNMENTS

A few Route 66–era motels remain on the east side of Pasadena. The Pasadia Motor Hotel, situated at 3625 East Colorado Boulevard, opened in the spring of 1959 and is still there today with the classic sign intact. "Pasadia" is a variation of Pasadena. Some of the luxury rooms even had private patios and kitchens. It also had a television in every room and advertised as being close to many "exquisite" restaurants.

Another classic sign remains in front of the Hi-Way Host Motel, 3474 East Colorado Boulevard. Constructed in 1957, the 40-room Hi-Way Host was rated as outstanding by AAA. In its accommodations guides, AAA noted that motels within a 20-mile radius of Pasadena charged higher rates in late December and early January because of the Rose Parade and Rose Bowl game and rooms usually had to be rented for at least several days.

The Bella Vista Motor Court, 3438 East Colorado Boulevard, is shown here in 1936. (Bella Vista means "beautiful view.") At that time, the rooms with a bath rented for $1.50 and up per night. It included 20 cottages and was later known as the Bella Vista Motel. Owners included George and Josephine Farmer, Charles Sanders, and Charlotte and Frank Karbiner. The motel closed in November 1962, and a GMC-Buick dealership is now located on the site.

It was a Pasadena architect, Arthur Heineman, who created the concept of the "motel," combining more than a single unit under one roof. He designed the first in the nation at San Luis Obispo, California, in 1925. The early auto courts, like the Gypsy Trail, were located in the nearly undeveloped eastern approach to Pasadena. Owner Stephen Hambaugh left in 1939 and became co-owner of the famous De-Anza Lodge on Route 66 in Albuquerque, New Mexico.

Floyd Gwinn ran the food service at the internment camp in Pasadena during World War II, serving over three tons of rice per day. On December 29, 1947, he opened Gwinn's Restaurant and Drive-In at 2915 East Colorado Boulevard. The stunning modern design was by Harold Zook and Harold Bissner. Gwinn served as mayor of Pasadena in 1965–1966. Gwinn's was in operation until 1972, and the site is now a luxury car service center.

Ace-Hi Motel
2870 E. Colorado St. (U.S. 66)
Pasadena 8, Calif.

In 1940, Route 66 was routed over East Colorado Boulevard through East Pasadena to connect with the Arroyo Seco Parkway. By the end of the 1940s, there were 13 new motels on East Colorado Boulevard. The former Ace-Hi Motel is the oldest still standing, constructed in 1946. The 12-unit property was owned by Lee Balaam at the time of this postcard. It is now known as the Ace Motel, and the vintage sign is still there.

Googie architecture was inspired by space-age aerodynamics, jets, and automobiles and was a popular style for coffeehouses, car washes, banks, and motels. The Astro Motels, including this location at 2818 East Colorado Boulevard, are outstanding examples. The chain also had locations in Barstow and San Bernardino, as well as at Kingman and Winslow, Arizona. The Pasadena location was built in 1962 and has been recently renovated.

Programmatic architecture, thematic structures intended to grab the attention of motorists, reached its peak in California. Walter C. Folland designed the Mother Goose Pantry, a two-story restaurant at 1951 East Colorado Boulevard in Pasadena. It opened in 1927. The waitresses could be no taller than five feet, two inches tall and weigh 112 pounds or less. A mechanical Mother Goose circled the huge shoe. Later named the Shoe Restaurant, it was gone by the early 1950s.

A lesson in architecture continues at 1855 East Colorado Boulevard. Draper's Studio of Modes, shown here in 1951, is an Art Deco design. The sleek and elegant style was popular from the 1920s to World War II. Draper's Studio of Modes was founded by Virginia Draper in 1927 and grew into a national chain of clothing stores, now Draper's and Damon's. The original building now houses medical professional offices. (Mike Ward.)

The Saga Motor Hotel at 1633 East Colorado Boulevard has been a landmark since 1959 and sits directly on the route of the Rose Parade. It was designed by Harold Zook, codesigner of Gwinn's Drive-In. Zook also designed the Van de Kamp's coffee shop with the windmill on top that became the landmark Denny's restaurant in Arcadia. The Saga has held up well and has been featured in the television shows *CSI* and *Dexter*.

Car culture took hold quickly in Pasadena. In 1915, the city had more automobiles per capita than any other in the world. There was one for every eight people, compared to the national average of one in 43. The Howard Motor Company Packard dealership, with its Churrigueresque ornamentations, opened in 1927 and still stands at 1285 East Colorado Boulevard. Listed in the National Register of Historic Places, the building housed auto dealerships until 2006.

After a brutal winter in 1873, a group of about 100 families from Indiana sent Dr. Daniel M. Berry to find property in Southern California where they could settle. Berry purchased 4,000 acres that were part of the Rancho del Rincon de San Pascual. He formed the Southern California Orange and Citrus Growers Association and sold stock to raise funds to bring the families to the colony. In 1875, they named it "Pa-sa-de-na," which is derived from the Chippewa for "crown of the valley." (Metro Library and Archive.)

Pasadena City Hall was completed on December 27, 1927, and the dome rises 206 feet. It can be seen in Charlie Chaplin's *The Great Dictator*, and outside Leonard and Sheldon's apartment on the television series *Big Bang Theory*. Viewers will also recognize it as the city hall of the fictional Pawnee City on *Parks and Recreation* and as the Beverly Hills Police Station in the *Beverly Hills Cop* films. A major renovation, as well as a seismic retrofit, was completed in 2007.

THE RAYMOND
PASADENA SOUTHERN CALIFORNIA

The Raymond was the first of the grand hotels that made Pasadena an attractive winter tourist destination. The four-story hotel atop Bacon Hill opened in 1886. It featured 200 guest rooms, 43 bathrooms, 40 water closets, and a 104-foot-tall tower. It burned down on Easter Sunday in 1895 but was rebuilt in 1901. The Raymond faded amid increased competition and closed in 1931 due to the Great Depression. It was demolished in 1934.

On January 1, 1890, the Valley Hunt Club of Pasadena launched the Tournament of Roses to promote Pasadena as the "Mediterranean of the West." At that time, it included chariot races, jousting, tug-of-war, and polo under the warm California sun. Carriages decorated in roses paraded down Colorado Boulevard before the tournament. The Rose Parade still takes place each year on New Year's Day or on January 2 if New Year's falls on a Sunday.

COLORADO STREET BRIDGE   PASADENA, CAL. 805

The majestic Colorado Street Bridge over the Arroyo Seco was dedicated on December 13, 1913, and carried Route 66 from 1935 until 1940. It is 148 feet tall at its highest point and is known as "Suicide Bridge." Over 150 people have jumped to their death from the span. Over half of those were prior to 1937, when the first barrier was erected. After nine more deaths in 2017, the city extended fencing along the entire length of the bridge.

VISTA DEL ARROYO HOTEL FROM COLORADO STREET BRIDGE   PASADENA, CAL. 806

Note the early suicide prevention barriers in this postcard view of the Colorado Street Bridge. The Vista del Arroyo Hotel is at right. Beginning in 1920, the Vista del Arroyo was built in stages. The War Department converted the former hotel into a hospital in 1943, and then it housed other federal agencies before restoration began in 1981. Today, the once luxurious hotel serves as the Richard H. Chambers US Court of Appeals.

93

The once glamorous Pasadena Winter Garden is now a storage facility. The Streamline Moderne rink on South Arroyo Parkway opened in 1940, and Olympic legend Peggy Fleming trained here early in her career. It was owned by real estate magnate Cliff Henderson, who cofounded the city of Palm Desert, California. After closing in 1966, it became a postal service facility. But the ground was still frozen, and the postal service moved out because the floor was too cold!

One of the first major tourist attractions in Southern California was in the Arroyo Seco Valley. In 1886, Edwin Cawston smuggled 50 ostriches from South Africa to establish his farm in Norwalk. Only 18 made it. But the herd grew, and in 1895, he opened Cawston's Ostrich Farm in South Pasadena. Tourists flocked to ride ostriches, enjoy ostrich carriage rides, and see the world's first commercial solar-powered motor. The farm closed in 1935. (South Pasadena Public Library.)

Original Route 66 headed south on Fair Oaks Avenue to Huntington Drive to North Broadway. The 1931–1934 alignment to Highland Park turned west from Fair Oaks onto Mission Street in front of a pharmacy that opened in 1915. Originally the South Pasadena Pharmacy, it was later named the Raymond Pharmacy and then the Fair Oaks Pharmacy. The Fair Oaks boasts a real soda fountain from a pharmacy in the Route 66 city of Joplin, Missouri. (Fair Oaks Pharmacy.)

The Rialto Theater on Fair Oaks Avenue in South Pasadena opened in 1925 and is one of the last surviving single-screen theaters in Southern California. The *Los Angeles Times* called the design by Lewis Arthur Smith "an odd mash up of Spanish Baroque and Egyptian kitsch." Smith also designed the nearby Highland Theater. The Rialto closed in 2007. Featured in the film *La La Land*, as of 2018 it was being used by a church group. (South Pasadena Library.)

Center of LOCKWOOD AUTO COURT · 70 Cottages

Follow North Broadway to Mission Road, then Right Two Blocks, or North Main Street to Zoo at End of Car Line.

LOCKWOOD AUTO COURT LOS ANGELES, CALIFORNIA

Just south of where original 66 turned from Mission Road onto North Broadway in Lincoln Heights, guests at the Lockwood Auto Court could hear lions roaring. The Selig Zoo was just across the road. The Los Angeles Ostrich Farm, the Los Angeles Alligator Farm, and Lincoln Park all drew tourists to the area. Lincoln Park was established in 1881. It was known as Eastlake Park for a time, and then renamed Lincoln Park again in 1917.

Entrance to the Selig Zoo, Eastlake Park, Los Angeles, Cal.

William Selig's Polyscope Studios housed its exotic animals at the world's largest private zoo on the north end of Eastlake, now Lincoln Park. Selig Zoo opened to the public in 1915. After the studio folded, it became the Luna Park Zoo, and then changed owners and names a couple of times before closing in 1940. Most of the animals were moved to Griffith Park. The gates and sculpted lions and elephants stood until the 1960s. Some of the restored lions now stand watch at the Los Angeles Zoo.

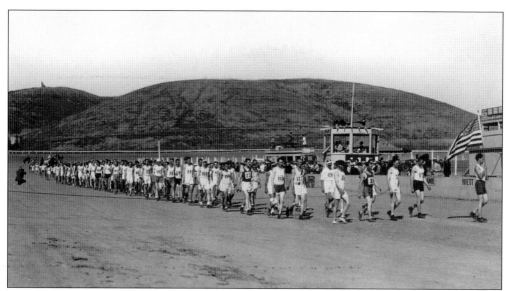

On March 4, 1928, 199 runners toed the line at Legion Ascot Speedway in Lincoln Heights to start the "Bunion Derby," a transcontinental footrace that put Route 66 on the front pages. Andy Payne, a half Cherokee from the Route 66 town of Foyil, Oklahoma, won the $25,000 grand prize. He made it to New York City in 573 hours, 4 minutes, and 34 seconds. Over two dozen drivers lost their lives at Ascot from 1924 until it burned in 1936. (Steve Rider.)

Until 1936, Route 66 crossed the Los Angeles River on the North Broadway Bridge, which opened in 1911 as the Buena Vista Viaduct. The span, with its Beaux-Arts details and Ionic columns on pedestals, was the longest and widest concrete bridge in California at the time. The North Broadway Bridge is the second oldest major span still in regular use on Route 66. It underwent a seismic retrofit and restoration in 2000. (University of Southern California Digital Archive.)

The York Boulevard Bridge over the Arroyo Seco is interesting because it carried one Route 66 alignment and now crosses over another. The 1931–1934 alignment crossed it between South Pasadena and Highland Park. The Arroyo Seco Parkway was constructed to run beneath the span and carried Route 66 from 1940 to 1964. The six-span reinforced concrete arch spandrel bridge was the first important concrete crossing of the Arroyo Seco and was constructed in 1912.

In Highland Park, the 1931–1934 and 1936–1940 routes followed North Figueroa Street past the Highland Theater. Silent film star Norma Shearer appeared on opening night in 1925. Vandalized and picketed for showing pornography, the Highland closed in 1975. The rooftop sign was relit in 2011 after an effort by the National Park Service Route 66 Corridor Preservation Program, residents, and neighborhood groups. The Highland now has three screens. (Highland Theater.)

"Chicken Boy" now roosts atop Future Studio and Design in Highland Park. Also known as the "Statue of Liberty of Los Angeles," he originally topped a restaurant at 454 South Broadway. Amy Inouye saved the icon when the restaurant closed in 1984. Chicken Boy is an adapted "Tall Guy," manufactured by International Fiberglass. Such figures were common on the American roadside and were used to advertise everything from mufflers and tires to hot dogs. (Future Studio.)

A 1935 Route 66 construction alignment used Colorado Boulevard west and then came through Eagle Rock to San Fernando Road. This short-lived route passed Albert Dejacomo's Auto Court at 1460 West Colorado Boulevard, now known as the Islander Motel. In 1936, Route 66 was changed to turn south from Colorado Boulevard onto Figueroa Street and back through Highland Park. That route became Alternate 66 when the Arroyo Seco Parkway was completed in 1940.

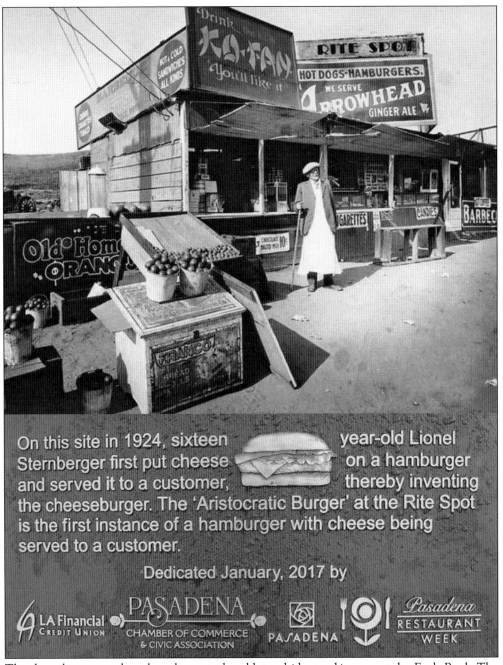

On this site in 1924, sixteen year-old Lionel Sternberger first put cheese on a hamburger and served it to a customer, thereby inventing the cheeseburger. The 'Aristocratic Burger' at the Rite Spot is the first instance of a hamburger with cheese being served to a customer.

Dedicated January, 2017 by

LA Financial CREDIT UNION   PASADENA CHAMBER OF COMMERCE & CIVIC ASSOCIATION   PASADENA   Pasadena RESTAURANT WEEK

The cheeseburger may have been born at a humble roadside stand in present-day Eagle Rock. The Pasadena Chamber of Commerce says it happened in 1924 at Herman Sternberger's Rite Spot at 1500 Colorado Boulevard, which later became an alignment of Route 66. A plaque erected in front of the present-day credit union acknowledges Herman's 16-year-old son Lionel Sternberger with the idea. It was then listed on the menu as the "Aristocratic Burger."

Six

Los Angeles

Since 1916, planners had envisioned a high-speed scenic parkway connecting Pasadena with Los Angeles along the banks of the Arroyo Seco. The Arroyo Seco Parkway was the first freeway in the West. The initial six-mile stretch opened on December 30, 1940, and was dedicated by Gov. Cuthbert Olsen. Olsen said the new route "has removed forever the creeping, fuming parade of choked up traffic between the two cities." (California Department of Transportation.)

The Figueroa Street Viaduct over the Los Angeles River, completed in 1937, allowed drivers to bypass the busy Broadway Bridge. Figueroa Street comes in at top left, and the future connection with the Arroyo Seco Parkway veers off to the right. The point where the parkway ended became a major traffic choke point until a southern extension was ready in 1943. The area at upper right remained undeveloped due to flooding until the channelization of the Arroyo Seco.

FIGUEROA TUNNELS   LOS ANGELES, CALIF.   'VI'C 51

In preparation for the planned high-speed route between downtown Los Angeles and Pasadena, four Art Deco tunnels were built to speed Figueroa Street beneath the hills of Elysian Park. The first three, between the Los Angeles River and Solano Avenue, opened in November 1931. The fourth and longest opened on August 4, 1936. The Figueroa Street Tunnels originally carried two-way traffic, which added to the bottleneck when the Arroyo Seco Parkway opened.

In 1941, crews began blasting away to ease the delays along the Arroyo Seco. A new bridge for southbound traffic was built next to the Figueroa Street Viaduct. Four new lanes were slashed through the hills at a higher elevation immediately west of the Figueroa Street Tunnels. The new lanes opened on December 30, 1943, but still fed into surface streets downtown. Northbound traffic was then shifted to use all four lanes of the tunnels and the Figueroa Street Viaduct.

As of September 22, 1953, the Arroyo Seco Parkway was extended two miles south to the famous four-level, or "stack," interchange connecting with the Hollywood Freeway, US 101. The Arroyo Seco Parkway became the Pasadena Freeway (CA 110) in 1954. In 2010, the state restored the original name. The parkway is not a leisurely drive today. Speeding drivers, congestion, narrow lanes, and short on-ramps create a hair-raising experience.

Dodger Stadium opened in 1962 on a site that was originally a Mexican American community named Chavez Ravine. The residents were forced out for a proposed housing project that was never built, and then the city sold the land to Dodgers owner Walter O'Malley. The stadium is the home of the Los Angeles Dodgers of the National League and has hosted a Mass conducted by Pope John Paul II and concerts by the Beatles, Michael Jackson, Elton John, and U2.

Once advertised as "In the center of LA and everything," the Paradise Motel still features some nice neon. Harvey Hanson opened the motel at 1116 West Sunset Boulevard in 1946 and it was operated by Norma and Harry Clayton at the time of this postcard. The Paradise was featured in an episode of the television show *The O.C.* substituting for a motel in Tijuana, Mexico. The tracks were used by Pacific Electric Red Cars serving Hollywood, a line abandoned in 1953–1954.

105

Los Angeles's original Chinatown was mostly demolished in 1933 for construction of Union Station. In 1938, socialite Christine Sterling created China City, a stereotypical Hollywood version a few blocks away. Chinese business owners, led by Peter Soo Hoo Sr., opened New China Town a few weeks later. Sterling's vision was destroyed by fire in 1939, and though it was rebuilt, it burned down again in 1949. New China Town still thrives today.

Union Station was built to consolidate the operations of the Southern Pacific, Union Pacific, and Atchison, Topeka, & Santa Fe Railroads. The father-son team of John and Donald Parkinson designed the station in Mission Moderne style and it opened in 1939. During World War II, 100 troop trains came through daily. Union Station is currently a hub for Metro, Metrolink, and Amtrak. It appeared in such films as *Blade Runner* and *The Dark Knight Rises*.

El Pueblo de Nuestra Señora la Reina de los Ángeles de Porciúncula, the Town of Our Lady the Queen of the Angels of Porciuncula, was officially founded on September 4, 1781. Olvera Street is a Mexican marketplace and major tourist attraction in El Pueblo de Los Ángeles Historic Monument. It was established in 1930 near the Avila Adobe, which was constructed in 1818. Olvera Street was the dream of Christine Sterling, who also created China City.

On August 15, 1926, an exclusive motel for female travelers and families, backed by the Young Women's Christian Association, opened its doors. The 400-room, 13-story European Mediterranean–style Hotel Figueroa soon began allowing male guests. It was designed by Stanton, Reed & Hibbard. The hotel at 930 South Figueroa Street underwent a $30 million remodeling completed in 2016.

Angel's Flight is a 298-foot-long narrow-gauge railway on the steep incline of Bunker Hill between Hill and Olive Streets. The two cars run in opposite directions on a shared cable. The original Angel's Flight ran from 1901 until 1969. Rebuilt a half-block away in 1996, it was closed from 2001 to 2010 and from 2013 to 2017 due to safety concerns. Angel's flight was featured on television on *Dragnet* and *Perry Mason* as well as in the 2016 film *La La Land*. (Library of Congress.)

Route 66 originally terminated at Seventh Street and Broadway in the heart of the Theater District. Looking west on Seventh Street, the 12-story Loew's State Theater at left opened in 1921. It closed in the 1990s and was leased to a church. It is now awaiting restoration. Bullock's Department Store was in business from 1906 until 1983. Bank of America occupied the Haas Building, built in 1915 and now converted to apartments.

Lavish movie palaces line Broadway in downtown LA. The Los Angeles Theater at left center was the most opulent. It opened on January 30, 1931, with the premiere of Charlie Chaplin's *City Lights*. Chaplin was unhappy when the film was stopped so management could brag about the theater. The theater has been featured in several television shows and films, including the two *Charlie's Angels* movies.

Ex-missionary Clifford Clinton founded his chain of cafeterias during the Great Depression and vowed no one would be turned away. Patrons paid what they could afford. Clifton's Brookdale at Seventh Street and Broadway was the last survivor, with its giant fake redwood tree and genuine meteorite on top of a bar fashioned from a church altar. Just a few years after a major renovation, the cafeteria portion was closed in 2018 to create the Exposition Marketplace, a high-end food hall.

The Broadway Tunnel through Fort Moore Hill eased congestion downtown by making Broadway a wide thoroughfare through to Buena Vista Street. Buena Vista later became Sunset Boulevard. Work began on November 2, 1899. The 760-foot-long tunnel opened on August 17, 1901, and was reconstructed in 1915. The north entrance to the tunnel is shown here in 1939. (California Historical Society.)

In 1936, Route 66 was extended from downtown over Sunset Boulevard to Santa Monica Boulevard. The section on Sunset Boulevard was replaced by the Hollywood Freeway in April 1954. Construction wiped out the Broadway Tunnel and Fort Moore Hill, where the town gallows once stood. The work created a canyon for the freeway, now known as "the Downtown Slot." This section is one of the worst traffic bottlenecks in the United States. (Los Angeles Public Library.)

Los Angeles City Hall was dedicated on April 26, 1928, and has been featured in dozens of movies and television shows, such as *Dragnet* and *Superman*. At 32 stories, it was the tallest in the city until 1964. During a seismic retrofit completed in 2001, the landmark was lifted from its foundation and placed on base isolators that would allow it to withstand an 8.1 magnitude earthquake. The building can slide up to 24 inches in any direction.

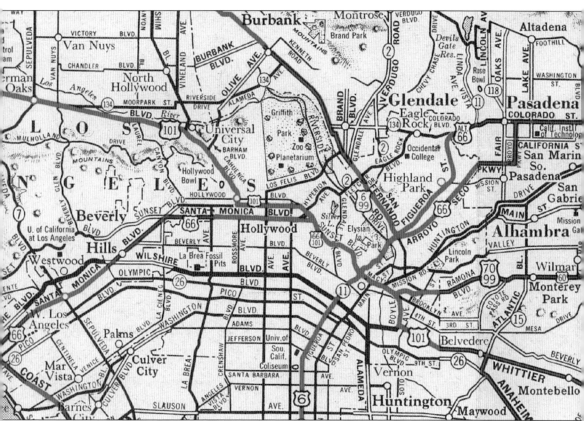

This Union 76 map of Los Angeles, issued in 1950, is a good reference to the alignments prior to construction of the freeways. The Route 66 mainline was routed over the Arroyo Seco Parkway while the alignment of Figueroa Street was Alternate 66. Streets that carried other alignments mentioned in this book can also be seen, including Fair Oaks Avenue, Mission Road, North Figueroa Street, Broadway, Huntington Drive, Sunset Boulevard, and the 1935 alignment through Eagle Rock.

Seven

HOLLYWOOD AND SANTA MONICA

The iconic Hollywood sign is visible from Santa Monica Boulevard. The original wooden sign on Mount Lee was erected in 1923 to promote the Hollywoodland real estate development. It was intended to only last about 18 months but became a symbol of the film industry. The last four letters were removed in 1949. *Playboy* magazine founder Hugh Hefner raised funds to replace the termite-riddled sign, and new enamel letters were unveiled on November 11, 1978.

Hollywood played a major role in creating the image of Route 66. While some of *The Grapes of Wrath* locations were on the road, much of the movie was shot on studio back lots. This famous promotional shot of the fictional Joad family overlooking the flourishing valley was taken on the Iverson Movie Ranch at Chatsworth. The shot that actually appeared in the movie was from a lower angle that eliminated the rocks. This location is preserved as a park.

A classic song assures that Route 66 will remain a pop culture icon. In 1946, Bobby Troup and his wife, Cynthia, left Pennsylvania for Hollywood. On the road in a 1941 Buick, bought with the royalty check for his first hit, "Daddy," Bobby considered writing a song about US 40. But Cynthia suggested "(Get Your Kicks on) Route 66." They arrived in Hollywood on February 14, and Nat King Cole recorded the song on March 15.

The television show *Route 66* made the road a symbol of freedom and adventure. On CBS from 1960 to 1964, the show followed a pair of drifters, Tod Stiles (Martin Milner) and Buz Murdock (George Maharis), in a Corvette. *On the Road* author Jack Kerouac considered suing when he saw the show. During the third season, Glenn Corbett as Lincoln Case replaced Maharis. The show seldom filmed on Route 66; this scene was shot at Lake Havasu, Arizona.

Visitors from around the world pay their respects to the legends at the Hollywood Forever Cemetery. The 62-acre cemetery on Santa Monica Boulevard is the final resting place of Judy Garland, Jayne Mansfield, Douglas Fairbanks, and many more stars. It was established in 1899, and 40 acres on the south end were sold in 1920 for construction of Paramount Studios. This photograph was taken during Rudolph Valentino's funeral in 1926. (Hollywood Forever.)

There is no telling what the teetotalling founders of Hollywood would think today. Kansas real estate baron Horace Wilcox and his wife, Daieda, planned a Christian community free from alcohol and other vices. Until 1910, actors were not allowed to stay the night in town. The famous corner of Hollywood Boulevard and Vine Street is one mile north of Route 66. Originally a pair of dirt streets, Hollywood Boulevard was Prospect Avenue and Vine Street was Weyse Avenue.

Grauman's Chinese Theater is a symbol of Hollywood. However, the film capital of the world could have been on Route 66 in Flagstaff, Arizona. In 1913, director Cecil B. DeMille came West to film *The Squaw Man* in Arizona. He did not like the light in Flagstaff, so his crew continued on. He also did not want to shoot in Edendale, where the early studios were located. So the crew rented a barn that still stands at Vine Street and Selma Avenue in Hollywood.

Icons such as Frank Sinatra, Elvis Presley, Clark Gable, and others frequented the Formosa Café, situated across from the Samuel Goldwyn Studios. It opened in the 1920s as a tiny diner, known as the Red Post Café. In 1939, Maximilian Goldstein expanded it into the Formosa Café and added a red Pacific Electric trolley car. The classic interior seen in the film *L.A. Confidential* was torn out before the café closed in 2016; however, a new ownership group restored it in 2018.

Located at Santa Monica and Crescent Heights Boulevards, the Kings Restaurant—"Where Hollywood Royalty Dines"—was endorsed in print by Errol Flynn and broadcaster Walter Winchell. Owned by Paul Franks and George Distel, it advertised "The only bona fide Eastern seafood house on the West Coast, specializing in Oysters Rockefeller." The seafood was flown in by American Airlines. Unfortunately, the owners went bankrupt in 1954.

Irv Gendis took over a hamburger stand at 8289 Santa Monica Boulevard in 1970 and named it Irv's Burgers. It became a hangout for rock stars such as Jim Morrison of The Doors, and was featured on the cover of a Linda Ronstadt album. Sonia Hong and her family bought the business in 2000 and, for years, battled the landowner's attempts to force them out so the site could be redeveloped. Sonia, Sean, and "Mama" Hong were forced to move a few blocks east in 2013. Irv's closed on November 24, 2018. (Jim Hinckley.)

John "Barney" Anthony brought Barney's Beanery from Berkeley to West Hollywood in 1927 when Santa Monica Boulevard was a dirt road. It became a favorite of Charlie Chaplin, Marilyn Monroe, Janis Joplin, and Jim Morrison. Irwin Held owned it from the early 1970s until 1998. Peter Falk was a regular, and it was featured often in his television series *Columbo*. Quentin Tarantino is said to have written much of *Pulp Fiction* at his favorite booth there. (Jim Hinckley.)

Future Hall of Famer and Dodgers pitcher Sandy Koufax bought the Tropicana Motel at 8585 Santa Monica Boulevard in 1962. Koufax sold it to a group led by Jerry Heiner, and it became popular with rockers. Janis Joplin, Alice Cooper, Bob Marley, Joan Jett, and the Ramones were just a few of the greats to stay there. The Tropicana was demolished in 1987 to make room for a new Ramada Inn and retail stores.

The Alta Cienega Motel at La Cienega and Santa Monica Boulevards also has a rock-and-roll pedigree. Jim Morrison of the Doors lived here from 1968 to 1970, and his favorite room was No. 32. Fans stay in the Jim Morrison Room and leave behind scrawled lyrics, poetry, and tributes that are painted over every couple of years. The Doors offices and studio were just down the street from "the green hotel," which is how it is referred to in the lyrics to "Celebration of the Lizard King."

Route 66 crosses Rodeo Drive, where the famous high-end shops are located, and Wilshire Boulevard, where the Beverly Hilton opened in 1955. Home of the Golden Globe Awards since 1961, the Hilton has seen its share of scandal. It was frequented by John F. Kennedy and Marilyn Monroe and used by the prostitution ring of Hollywood madam Heidi Fleiss. Whitney Houston died in a luxury suite bathtub at the Beverly Hilton in 2012.

Burton Green developed a subdivision in 1907 and named it after Beverly Farms, Massachusetts. Landscape architect Wilbur Cook laid out the first streets. Movie stars began migrating to Beverly Hills after Douglas Fairbanks and Mary Pickford bought their "Pickfair" estate in 1919. Will Rogers was an honorary mayor. Erected in 1911, the sign in Beverly Gardens Park on Santa Monica Boulevard was recreated in 2014. (Beverly Hills Historical Society.)

ELECTRIC COLOR FOUNTAIN   BEVERLY HILLS, CAL. 675

The beautiful Beverly Hills Electric Color Fountain at Santa Monica and Wilshire Boulevards was dedicated in 1931. At the west end of Beverly Gardens Park, the fountain features a representation of a Tongva Native American on top. The multicolored lights and water jets create 60 different effects. The fountain underwent a restoration in 2016. It appears in the 1995 movie *Clueless* and in the Go-Go's music video for "Our Lips are Sealed."

Plans to construct a Church of Latter Day Saints temple atop a rise overlooking Santa Monica Boulevard were announced in 1937, but it was 1951 before ground was broken. Dedicated on March 11, 1956, the 190,614-square-foot structure is second only to the Salt Lake City temple in size. The spire is 257 feet tall and is topped with a 16.5-foot gold statue of the angel Moroni. It sits on 13 acres of beautiful grounds. (Los Angeles Public Library.)

On St. Monica's day, May 4, 1769, Spanish explorer Gaspar de Portola and his party came upon two springs and called the place Santa Monica. Col. Robert S. Baker and Nevada senator John P. Jones auctioned the first lots on July 15, 1875. They built a railroad to Los Angeles and a 4,700-foot-long pier. Their hopes that it would become the Port of Los Angeles were not realized, but that helped Santa Monica keep its charm. The population exploded in the 1920s.

The William Tell Motel and Apartments was advertised as "California's Largest and Finest Family Motel." The complex had 110 units covering five acres on Santa Monica Boulevard near Twenty-sixth Street. It was operated by Mr. and Mrs. Roy Plater and later by Bert Olden, who also owned the nearby Red Apple Motel on Wilshire Boulevard. The William Tell complex closed in late 1975, and the site became a CVS pharmacy.

Eight

END OF THE TRAIL

From 1935 to 1964, Route 66 ended shy of the ocean at the intersection of Lincoln and Olympic Boulevards. Officially, all US highways have to intersect with another US route, in this case 101 Alternate. The Penguin Coffee Shop, a 1959 Googie design by Armet Davis Newlove Architects, is now a Mel's Drive-In location. Mel's is a chain that started in San Francisco and was made famous in the film *American Graffiti*. (Caltrans.)

The vast majority of Route 66 travelers will continue on Santa Monica Boulevard to the sea. For over 40 years, the Art Deco Bay Cities Guaranty Building at right was the tallest in Santa Monica. The 12-story structure with its stepped clock tower was designed by Albert Walker and Percy Eisen and opened in January 1930 just before Bay Cities collapsed in the wake of the stock market crash. The landmark has undergone extensive renovation and retrofitting.

Almost immediately after the death of Will Rogers, a movement was started to dedicate US 66 in his honor. In 1935, the US Highway 66 Association designated Route 66 as the Will Rogers Highway. The association unveiled a new emblem, seen here at Palisades Park on August 17, 1937. From left to right are actress Rochelle Hudson, Will's son Bill Rogers, Gov. Frank Merriam, and humorist and author Irvin S. Cobb. (Steve Rider.)

Fifteen-year-old starlet Linda Ware greets Santa Monica mayor Claude C. Crawford at the Will Rogers Memorial Highway Association convention in July 1940. Born Beverly Jane Stillwagon, she was sent to an orphanage at age four after her mother died. Her aunt and uncle later brought her to Hollywood and her father sued for custody when she landed a movie deal. He lost the case when the girl testified that he "never bought me so much as an ice cream cone."

In 1952, an eight-state caravan rededicated Route 66 as the Will Rogers Highway to promote the movie *The Story of Will Rogers*. Signs marking the designation were placed at each state line along the way. On July 1, 1952, the final marker was placed beneath the palm trees in Palisades Park across from the intersection of Santa Monica Boulevard and Ocean Avenue. From there, it was just two blocks to the Santa Monica Pier.

On September 9, 1909, the Santa Monica Municipal Pier opened to the public. The pier was originally constructed to carry sewage out to sea. Carousel maker Charles Looff developed the amusement pier and hippodrome with its famous carousel in 1916. The La Monica Ballroom opened in 1924. It was the largest in the world at the time, but its dance hall days ended during the Great Depression. The La Monica became a skating rink and was demolished in 1963.

The famous neon "Santa Monica Yacht Harbor" sign was added when a new ramp to the pier opened in 1940. The City of Santa Monica proposed demolishing the pier in 1973, and it was badly damaged by a storm in 1983. But by 1990, the seaside icon had been reconstructed, and the carousel was rebuilt inside the Looff Hippodrome. In 1996, Pacific Park opened, the first full-fledged amusement park on the pier since the 1930s.

In 1935, a movie studio erected a sign reading, "End of the Trail," on the bluffs overlooking the Santa Monica Pier, which added to the public's perception that Route 66 ended at the ocean. Dan Rice opened the 66 to Cali shop on the Santa Monica Pier and then brought the Route 66 Alliance group and the city together to help him erect a replica of the sign. It was unveiled on November 11, 2009, and is now a popular photo op site. (Steve Rider.)

At the very end of the Santa Monica Pier, a display in a shop window memorializes Bob Waldmire, the artist and free spirit who inspired many to travel Route 66. Waldmire passed away on December 16, 2009. This is a place to reflect on one's journey on the road and through life. Route 66 travelers often stand at the end of the pier for a moment as the sun sinks beneath the waves. They sigh and slowly turn toward home. (Santa Monica Pier.)

DISCOVER THOUSANDS OF LOCAL HISTORY BOOKS FEATURING MILLIONS OF VINTAGE IMAGES

Arcadia Publishing, the leading local history publisher in the United States, is committed to making history accessible and meaningful through publishing books that celebrate and preserve the heritage of America's people and places.

Find more books like this at
www.arcadiapublishing.com

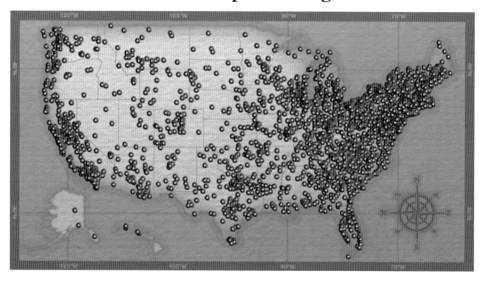

Search for your hometown history, your old stomping grounds, and even your favorite sports team.

Consistent with our mission to preserve history on a local level, this book was printed in South Carolina on American-made paper and manufactured entirely in the United States. Products carrying the accredited Forest Stewardship Council (FSC) label are printed on 100 percent FSC-certified paper.

MADE IN THE USA